D1541780

FUTURISM

A Modern Focus

FUTURISM

A Modern Focus

THE LYDIA AND HARRY LEWIS WINSTON COLLECTION

Dr. and Mrs. Barnett Malbin

THE SOLOMON R. GUGGENHEIM MUSEUM, NEW YORK

Published by

The Solomon R. Guggenheim Foundation

New York, 1973

Library of Congress

Card Catalogue Number: 73-86860

© The Solomon R. Guggenheim Foundation, 1973

Printed in the U.S.A.

Table of Contents

The Solomon R. Guggenheim Foundation

PRESIDENT   Peter O. Lawson-Johnston

TRUSTEES   H. H. Arnason, Eleanor Countess Castle Stewart,
                 Joseph W. Donner, Mason Welch Gross, Henry Allen Moe,
                 A. Chauncey Newlin, Mrs. Henry Obre, Daniel Catton Rich,
                 Albert E. Thiele, Michael F. Wettach, Carl Zigrosser.

The Solomon R. Guggenheim Museum

DIRECTOR   Thomas M. Messer

STAFF   Henry Berg, Deputy Director; Linda Konheim, Administrative Officer;
                 Agnes R. Connolly, Auditor; Susan L. Halper, Administrative Assistant;
                 John P. Rafferty, Managerial Assistant.

                 Louise Averill Svendsen, Curator; Diane Waldman, Curator of Exhibitions;
                 Margit Rowell, Curator of Special Exhibitions; Carol Fuerstein, Editor;
                 Linda Shearer, Research Fellow; Mary Joan Hall, Librarian; Ward Jackson,
                 Archivist; Cheryl McClenney, Sabine Rewald, Coordinators.

                 Orrin Riley, Conservator; Lucy Belloli, Assistant Conservator;
                 Saul Fuerstein, Preparator; Robert E. Mates, Photographer; Susan Lazarus,
                 Assistant Photographer; David Roger Anthony, Registrar; Elizabeth M. Fung
                 Cherie A. Summers, Assistant Registrars; Dana Cranmer, Coordinator.

                 Anne B. Grausam, Officer, Public Affairs; Miriam Emden, Members'
                 Representative; Darrie Hammer, Information; Carolyn Porcelli, Coordinator

                 Peter G. Loggin, Building Superintendent; Guy Fletcher, Jr.,
                 Assistant Building Superintendent; Charles F. Banach, Head Guard.

East end of Malbin home, from garden

Mr. and Mrs. Harry L. Winston boarding Queen Elizabeth, 1951, Cherbourg, France. In package is Severini's *Sea = Dancer*

Preface and Acknowledgements

Meaningful collecting is both object and idea bound. Neither "taste" operating in a conceptual vacuum, nor "systems" that arrange items within a preconceived pattern will yield live and rewarding results. The former tends to produce capricious fragments, the latter translates the objectives of the stamp collector into an area where these do not apply. Dr. and Mrs. Barnett Malbin's *Lydia and Harry Lewis Winston Collection* avoided both pitfalls from the outset. Harry and Lydia Winston, who started the collecting process many years ago, and Dr. Barnett Malbin who, at Lydia's side, continued the work in recent years, were all committed to an attentive scrutiny of individual works as well as to a functional placement of such works within the collection as a whole. It is this parallel awareness that determined the authority of the effort and the quality of the result.

The key concept in the Winston Collection is Futurism; and it is the quantity and quality of Futurist works that confer a particular status upon the collection and that assure its distinctiveness and character. But Futurism in the Winston Collection merely provides the main accent. Cubism and Purism, Dada and Surrealism, as well as some European and American currents of the post-war era are not only represented but have become an integral part of a visual unity, in fact, a study in visual relationships between styles of modern art. Boccioni, Balla, and Severini—the great trio of Futurist artists—are represented by key examples in various media, and in relatively large numbers. The Italian contingent is rounded out by the painters Russolo, Carra and Sironi and the sculptor Medardo Rosso. From this Italian core, the collection moves easily into Cubism where Picasso, Braque, Léger and Gris are supported by Delaunay, de La Fresnaye and Gleizes. In a different direction the Futurist center radiates toward Dada and Surrealism, as witnessed by a group of carefully chosen Schwitters, some Arp sculptures and works on paper, Max Ernst, Picabia and a marvelous Miró oil. The Guggenheim selection here attempts to follow the collection's impartiality toward medium. Archipenko is shown in works on paper as is Max Ernst, while the sculptors Brancusi, Calder, Giacometti, Lachaise, Laurens, Moore and Pevsner are represented by their most characteristic three-dimensional achievements. While the Winston Collection remains, for the most part, a grouping of European modernists of the now classical phase, post-war developments are by no means neglected. Tobey, Pollock, Louis, Noland and Stella represent an important segment of the collection's American holdings while Appel, Jorn, and Corneille, as well as examples from the School of Paris, furnish the European counterpart.

Those who create objects, or shape words into meaningful expressions or those who aim for tonal resolutions, are mirror makers. Their need is to fashion something that will return their own image, something that will allow them to see themselves in the reflection of their work. This common need for mirrors is by no means restricted to artists, unless we use "artist" in the broad sense of creative man at large. An art collection becomes a composite art-form when shaping instincts are translated into formal entities. In works of art, as in the collecting process, the capacity for ordering is rare, and objects therefore mostly remain devoid of meaning just as object assemblages fail to achieve significance. Exceptions to this situation are therefore particularly satisfying. Dr. and Mrs. Barnett Malbin's *Lydia and Harry Lewis Winston Collection* exemplifies an attainment of the collector's clear and positive mirror-image that is the result of authentic involvement and of serious, knowledgeable striving.

I am grateful to the numerous individuals within and outside the Guggenheim Museum who have been involved in the organization and presentation of the exhibition and its accompanying catalogue. In particular I would like to thank Linda Shearer, Research Fellow at the Guggenheim, who has worked on all phases of the project, assisted in the selection of works for the exhibition and contributed an essay to the catalogue. Also central to the success of the undertaking was the participation of Marianne W. Martin, Professor at New York University and author of the second catalogue essay. Mrs. Martin's special knowledge of Futurism made her generous advice invaluable to us. Ellen Sharp and Paul Binai of the Graphics Department of the Detroit Institute of Arts assisted with the Boccioni drawings and Jane Hickey, who has kept Lydia Malbin's extensive records up to date, has also been most helpful. Marianne Martin, in turn, expresses her gratitude to Joan M. Lukach of Cambridge, Massachusetts and Piero Pacini of Florence for their help, while Linda Shearer is indebted to William A. Camfield, Houston and to Sidney Geist, New York for clarifying matters of scholarly importance. The entire Guggenheim staff has contributed its time and skills and the following should be singled out for their direct participation: Roger Anthony, Carol Fuerstein, Linda Konheim, Beverly Liftman, Sabine Rewald and Orrin Riley.

THOMAS M. MESSER, DIRECTOR
The Solomon R. Guggenheim Museum

Dr. and Mrs. Barnett Malbin in Library of Malbin home

Beyond Futurism: The Winston/Malbin Collection

Lydia Winston Malbin grew up in Detroit in an atmosphere of devotion to the highest cultural aims. Her father was the innovative industrial architect Albert Kahn (1869-1949). He amassed an important library of rare books and filled his home with art; his greatest architectural achievements, like the Packard Motor Car Co. (1903-05) and the Chrysler Corporation de Soto Press Shop (1936), foreshadow much contemporary architecture. His daughter's collection demonstrates her own particular understanding of the forces of the twentieth century. Its encyclopedic scope reflects the numerous creative responses to the unique demands of our time.

Surrounded by art from childhood, it was not until the late 1930's that Mrs. Malbin began to collect seriously. In 1938 she had the good fortune to meet Alfred Stieglitz, who then had his American Place Gallery. He discussed modern art with her at great length and encouraged her burgeoning taste for the abstract. Among the first modern works she acquired were two Marins, two Feiningers, a Chagall and a Soutine which represent her early interest in both American and European art. By 1945 Mrs. Malbin had come into contact with Rose Fried, whose Pinacotheca Gallery eventually became the Rose Fried Gallery, which she often visited when she was in New York. Mrs. Malbin frequently acknowledges Mrs. Fried's important role in the formation of her collection: she had championed Arp, van Doesburg, Gabo, Kandinsky, Lissitzky, Mondrian, Picabia and Schwitters at a very early time. As the body of works grew, so did its scope. Yet, remarkably, despite the increasing range, a distinct direction began to emerge, for the collection evolved into one of the finest collections of Futurism extant.

Arp understood the fullness and diversity of the Winston/Malbin collection when he said:

> At the one pole the Winston collection contains works whose beauty has not been touched by the eternal transformation of the ephemeral. Among those I would include the works of Mondrian, van Doesburg, Albers, Freundlich, Herbin, Lissitsky, Pevsner and Gabo. At the opposite pole are to be found Boccioni, Masson, Pollock and Schwitters.[1]

Arp implicitly poses the question of whether it is possible for the apparent opposition to be resolved. Can Arp and Albers or Miró and Mondrian co-exist with their dissimilarities of intention and inspiration, which extend to the point of openly stated antagonisms of the esthetic sensibility? Can an awareness of twentieth-century art be revealed through a seemingly chaotic assembly of work? Arp seems to be emphasizing precisely the *potential* for such contradiction between the two fundamentally different approaches — romantic/classical, open/closed, multiple/unified, the commitedly political/the purely esthetic. A confrontation of this nature is central to the Futurists' art; from such a collision a synthesis emerges to form a higher vision.

> Let us leave Wisdom behind like a horrible mine ... Let us throw ourselves to be devoured by the Unknown, not because we are desperate, but simply to enrich the bottomless reservoirs of the Absurd.
>
> F. T. Marinetti, 1909[2]

1. Jean Arp, "Serious and Droll Speculations," *Collecting Modern Art,* exhibition catalogue, Detroit Institute of Art, 1957-58, p. 28
2. F. T. Marinetti, "First Futurist Manifesto," quoted in Marianne W. Martin, *Futurist Art and Theory: 1909-1915,* Clarendon Press, Oxford, 1968, p. 40

One must start with the central nucleus of the object one wants to create, in order to discover the new forms which connect it invisibly and mathematically to the visible plastic infinite *and to the* interior plastic infinite. *The new plasticity will thus be the translation in plaster, bronze, glass, wood, or any other material, of atmospheric planes that link and intersect things. What I have called* physical transcendentalism *can render plastically the sympathies and mysterious affinities which produce the reciprocal and formal influences of the objects' planes.*

Umberto Boccioni, 1912[3]

The range of Futurist theories opened up countless areas for other artists. The Dada and Surrealist movements developed directly out of ideas such as those expressed by Marinetti, while the Russian Constructivists were able to actualize what Boccioni had vehemently advocated but never realized in full. The international repercussions of the Futurists are due largely to their proselytizing manifestos and lecture tours. In addition, it has been observed that Boccioni's 1913 sculpture exhibition in Paris seems to have left an impression on a variety of artists: see Brancusi's *Prodigal Son*, 1915, Duchamp-Villon's *The Horse*, 1914, Archipenko's *Boxers*, 1913, all of which evidence a new element of dynamic and assymetrical thrusts of space and mass.[4] But without doubt, the greatest impact of Futurism occurs in the two seemingly opposed movements of Dada/Surrealism on the one hand, and of Constructivism on the other.

The initial Futurist movement was cut short by World War I; by 1916 Dada had grown out of it. Artists reacted in various ways to pressures exerted by the War. The Futurists had welcomed War enthusiastically since they felt it heralded the destruction of all traditional values. However the Dadaists' social point of view is negative and cynical: war and its attendant death and devastation is to them one expression of society's decay. In Germany particularly, where the economic depression was most severe, the Dada spirit was most active. Dadaists like Arp, Ernst and Schwitters in Germany and Duchamp and Picabia in New York and Paris created an art form as revolutionary as the Futurists had—an idiom which was a unique expression of the period. Irreverence and love of nonsense, blasphemy and political activism exists in both Dada and Futurism, tying them together on one level.

On a more substantial level, the two movements are related by an overriding faith in the artist's intuitive powers. Reinforced in part by the philosophy of Bergson and Nietzsche, men like Arp, Ernst and Schwitters recognized the need to return to a near-primary state in order to establish a non-static viewpoint that encouraged the artist's most personal expression and reflected the fluctuating and changing nature of life. Arp evolved one such solution. Speaking of his and Sophie Taueber's work of c.1915, Arp wrote:

We rejected everything that was copy or description, and allowed the Elementary and Spontaneous to react in full freedom. Since the disposition of planes, and the proportions and colors of these planes seemed to depend purely on chance, I declared that these works, like nature, were ordered "according to the law of chance," chance being for me merely a limited part of an unfathomable raison d'être, of an order inaccessible in its totality.[5]

Not only is Arp's work associated with nature through eternal laws contributing to its creation, but also through his particular type of abstraction, whose organic configurations recall and suggest foliage or animal life. Pre-dating Surrealist automatic writing, Arp's spontaneous approach re-

3. Umberto Boccioni, *"Technical Manifesto of Futurist Sculpture,"* reprinted in *Modern Artists on Art*, ed. Robert L. Herbert, Prentice-Hall, New Jersey, 1964, p. 51
4. See Sidney Geist, *Brancusi: A Study of The Sculpture*, Grossman, New York, 1968, pp. 149-150
5. Jean Arp, *On My Way: Poetry and Essays, 1912-1947*, Wittenborn, New York, 1948, p. 40

veals a profound grasp of his inner powers. His unique biomorphic shapes recur in both Miró and Calder (cat. nos. 68, 34) who also create a world based on imagination unrelated to objectively perceived reality. Because of Arp's emphasis on fantasy and the spontaneous workings of the mind, his art functions on multiple levels of association; certain shapes quite literally metamorphose into others, simultaneously altering and expanding their original connotations. These image transformations parallel the states and processes of the mind which preoccupied Arp. He found a subtle and abstract style to express these ideas — ideas which had been more explicitly handled by Russolo in *Perfume*, c. 1909 (cat. no. 93).

By 1919, Arp was working closely with Ernst in Cologne where they established an alternative to the far more political Dada contingent based in Berlin. Ernst, too, was concerned with the metamorphosis or multiple identity of images. But he, for the most part, uses absolutely realistic objects arranged in specific, and often ironic, relation to one another. The collage *Sitting Buddha* (cat. no. 38) is a humorous vision of the subject put together from biological drawings and reveals Ernst's peculiar sense of juxtaposition which later had great impact on Surrealism. Although their work assumed very different forms, Arp and Ernst's sensibilities were remarkably alike. Ernst endeavored to explore his mind's apparatus as freely as possible by means of "frottage." Frottage is a process, named in 1925 by Ernst, based on the traditional technique of rubbing. Ernst was no doubt encouraged in his quest for such a method by Breton's 1924 *Surrealist Manifesto*. Ernst has described the events which led to his discovery of this revelatory procedure.

> *Beginning with a memory of childhood . . . in the course of which a panel of false mahogany, situated in front of my bed, had played the role of optical* provocateur *of a vision of half-sleep, and finding myself one rainy evening in a seaside inn, I was struck by the obsession that showed to my excited gaze the floor-boards upon which a thousand scrubbings had deepened the grooves. I decided then to investigate the symbolism of this obsession and, in order to aid my meditative and hallucinatory faculties, I made from the boards a series of drawings by placing on them, at random, sheets of paper which I undertook to rub with black lead. In gazing attentively at the drawings thus obtained . . . I was surprised by the sudden intensification of my visionary capacities and by the hallucinatory succession of contradictory images superimposed, one upon the other, with the persistence and rapidity characteristic of amorous memories.*[6]

Both *Come Into the Continents* and the oil *Composition* (cat. nos. 40, 39) were made in this manner, demonstrating his unique insight into a fantasy world quite unlike Arp's. Appropriately, Arp wrote the introduction to Ernst's 1926 *Natural History*, a portfolio of his frottage drawings (an edition of which is in the collection). *Come Into the Continents* is related to two of this portfolio's plates. In his introduction, Arp incorporated the actual titles from the drawings — "enter the continents without knocking but with a muzzle of filligree."[7]

Both artists foreshadowed the Surrealist movement in which they were active participants by 1924. The Surrealist insistence on "pure psychic automatism" and "the omnipotence of the dream" obviated, to a certain extent, that quality of spontaneity which characterizes the early Arp and Ernst. This lack of spontaneity on the part of the Surrealist painters largely resulted from the influence of Breton, who extolled conscious control of the unconscious. Moreover, Breton's literary background undoubtedly set the stage for a movement less oriented toward the visual. Nevertheless, Miró's paintings of the 20's, like *Personage* (cat. no. 68), and Tanguy's work in his best known man-

6. Max Ernst, *Beyond Painting*, Wittenborn, New York, 1948, p. 7
7. Arp, *op. cit.*, p. 38

ner, like *Shadow Country* (cat. no. 108), represent two of the more visual aspects of the movement. Miró's abstract, biomorphic forms floating in an infinite azure space constitute an image which contrasts dramatically with Tanguy's precisely rendered dream-like and abstracted shapes grounded in a landscape setting. While Miró and Tanguy developed respectively the poetic/magical and the subconscious/dream-like tendencies of Surrealism, Masson (cat. no. 65), abandoned himself to the powers of automatism which enabled him to utilize to the fullest extent his intuitive sense of line and tension. The elements of chance, of accident, of randomness and coincidence have, of course, always played a certain part in the creative process. The Dadaists, however, impelled by the Futurists, made these elements more integral to their work to create a more dynamic art.

Another artist who, like the Futurists, strove vigorously to break down the barriers between discrete states of mind and precise points of termination was Kurt Schwitters (cat. nos. 94-98). Working out of a Cubist-Futurist impetus, he exemplifies the artist who totally and absolutely integrates object with background, life with art. Schwitters, who developed his own exuberant form of Dada in Hanover called "Merz" (from *Kommerzbank),* was a poet, as was Arp. Perhaps their propensity toward other art forms enabled them to be more open and expansive in the plastic arts and less concerned with the purely formal. The Futurists had been greatly involved with concrete poetry and carried over the use of words, sounds and letters into their art. These concerns are also very much a part of Schwitters' work. Although Schwitters' delicate collages and frequently less gentle constructions are based on well-composed Cubist structural formats, his unorthodox use of materials—personal possessions, discarded scraps and refuse culled from the streets—expanded Boccioni's concept of new materials creating a new reality:

Transparent planes, glass, sheets of metal, wires, external or internal electric lights can indicate the planes, inclinations, tones and halftones of a new reality . . .[8]

Why, then, should sculpture remain shackled by laws which have no justifications? Let us break them courageously and proclaim the complete abolition of the finished line and the closed statue. Let us open up the figure like a window and enclose within it the environment in which it lives. *Let us proclaim that the environment must form part of the plastic block as a special world regulated by its own laws.*[9]

Although Boccioni had advanced such theories, he still clung, in practice, to the figure as subject. Schwitters furthered the Futurist proclivity toward the fusion of sculptural object and environment through the destruction of traditional definitions of line, mass and space. Starting in the 1920's, Schwitters fabricated the *Merzbau,* which was built into his house in Hanover. It was an accretion of objects which proliferated and changed daily, growing over the years into a huge all-encompassing sculptural structure. In the course of his career, he built three of these; he worked on the second between 1937 and 1940 in Norway, while the third was begun in 1941 in England. These constructions, now destroyed, were the fulfillment of his ideal of total inclusiveness. Schwitters' accumulated environment represented something very different from the Futurist concept of fast-moving modern Europe. The age of technology had not left a positive impression on him; its waste products rather than its achievements consumed his interest.

Certain Dadaists did not ignore the fact that the machine age had spawned them. The Dada obsession with thought processes and states of mind was translated through the exploration of chance and accident into a kind of psychic mechanism. Picabia's *Alarm Clock I* (cat. no. 79) is a

---

8. Quoted in Martin, *op. cit.,* p. 127
9. Reprinted in Herbert, *op. cit.,* p. 54

superb synthesis of Dada methods of chance and a machine esthetic. Arp witnessed the making of this piece in Zurich where he met Picabia for the first time in 1919. Dismantling the clock in his hotel room, with the impetuosity for which he was famous, Picabia dipped its parts in ink, placed the inked elements on paper to leave an image, and then added a few lines to hold the composition together. The rashness of the esthetic decision combined with the reassembled, now useless clock expresses the artist's irreverent attitude toward technology and, even more, his ability to transform and break down a mechanical object so that its inner workings are fully revealed.

Duchamp and Picabia well understood that the machine which makes "things" work could be an apt metaphor for the workings (or non-workings) of all "things," even humans. The fact that Picabia depicted Marie Laurencin and the dancer Napierkowska (cat. nos. 78, 77) as non-functional mechanical beings confirms a sense of extreme ambiguity and irony. Both these female apparatuses could perform effectively if they were "turned on," but neither one would perform a concrete, logical function. Both works imply self-contained revolving movement, rather than directional thrust. Moreover, Napierkowska slightly resembles a spinning top, which is what she must have looked like to her audiences. These portraits have ceased to represent an external reality, rather they exist as specific, self-referential fantasy-realities.

The Dada sense of the mechanical age is far removed from the Constructivist sense; yet, both movements were passionately concerned with revealing the laws which govern universal processes. Dada machines are odd, magical, often anthropomorphic and sometimes sinister. The Constructivists never depicted actual machines, but rather attempted to utilize and incorporate real technology to create an art in keeping with the times, times in which they had ultimate faith. Their efforts to surpass external reality in order to arrive at the universal were imbued with a great sense of optimism and enthusiasm, resulting from both the innumerable esthetic possibilities which flowed from the new technology and from the volatile political atmosphere in Russia immediately following the 1917 revolution. Gabo and Pevsner, two Constructivists who figure prominently in the Winston/Malbin collection, both actively absorbed and expanded the basic tenets of Futurist theory in a way quite unlike the Dadaists. Their *Realist Manifesto*, written in 1920 at the height of cooperation between all branches of art and technology in Russia, defines their position vis-à-vis Futurism:

1. *To communicate the reality of life, art should be based on the two fundamental elements: space and time.*
2. *Volume is not the only spatial concept.*
3. *Kinetic and dynamic elements must be used to express the real nature of time; static rhythms are not sufficient.*
4. *Art should stop being imitative and try instead to discover new forms.*[10]

The use of the word "realist" has Platonic implications. Gabo and Pevsner propose that their art is founded on the same fundamental and invisible laws of energy and tension as those of the universe itself. Their sculpture constitutes its own world, never imitating or referring to an external reality. The concept of harmony is central and is predicated on an ever-changing and actively regenerative reality.

Boccioni's remarks furnish insight into Gabo and Pevsner's emphasis on space and time in sculpture:

In sculpture as well as in painting, one can renew art only by seeking the style of movement, *that is, by forming systematically and definitely into a synthesis that which Impression-*

10. Quoted in *Gabo-Pevsner,* The Museum of Modern Art, New York, 1948, p. 10

ism offered in a fragmentary, accidental, and consequently analytical way. The systematization of the vibration of light and of the interpenetrations of planes will produce Futurist sculpture: it will be architectonic in character, not only from the point of view of the construction of the masses, but also because the sculptural block will contain the architectonic elements of the sculptural milieu in which the subject lives."[11]

The Russian Constructivists created an art based on the renunciation of mass and the subsequent opening up of space; line was articulated as direction of force and energy, rather than as description. Time was introduced by means of actual and implied movement, capable of defining the space within which the motion occurred. The Dadaists embodied time in their work in a more cerebral and gestural fashion since a certain duration of time often determined the precise form a work of art assumed. Constructions like Tatlin's complex revolving *Monument to the Third International* of 1920, (never executed in final form) incorporated time as movement in both symbolic and actual forms. The Futurists had articulated the need for a "style of movement," but they integrated it into their paintings and sculpture primarily on a narrative level.

Gabo and Pevsners' investigations of motion, though based on an extension of Futurist inspiration, nevertheless stood for a radical departure. Gabo has described the inherent distinctions:

Ask any Futurist how he imagines speed, and on the scene will appear a whole arsenal of raging automobiles, rumbling stations, tangled wire, the clang, bang, noise and ring of the whirling streets . . . . This is not at all required for speed and its rhythms . . . . Look at a ray of sun—the quietest of the silent strengths—it runs three thousand kilometers in a second. Our starry sky —does anyone hear it?[12]

Pevsner expressed equally vehement feelings about the Futurist actualization of theories on movement:

In the field of painting the task of Futurism went no further than revised attempts to affix on canvas the optical reflex. . . . It is clear to anyone that we cannot re-create motion through a single graphic record of a series of snapshots of arrested movement.[13]

The Constructivists did not seek to transform the human figure into a mechanized robot; instead, in their hands, the figure becomes a form of interacting geometric solids and voids, as in Pevsner's Cubist-derived copper *Figure* of 1925 (cat. no. 74). The far-reaching effects of Cubism are apparent in both Futurism and Constructivism, but the latter movement more accurately represents a synthesis of the other two. Dependence on Cubist formal innovations, such as constructed objects and the incorporation of unorthodox materials,[14] combined with the realization of Futurist concepts in relation to energy, motion and the breakdown of mass contributed to the uniqueness of the Constructivist style.

Figure, like Gabo's earlier works of a similar style, has been split open to reveal its invisible workings—not in a biological, individual sense, but in a cosmological, ideal one. In spirit, their abstract constructions correspond to works by the mature Mondrian (cat. no. 69) who also was not concerned with representing externals, but with the creation of a self-contained reality encompassing the delicate balances and contradictions of a total cosmology. By 1922, Gabo, Pevsner,

11. Reprinted in Herbert, *op. cit.,* p. 53

12. Quoted in *Gabo-Pevsner, op. cit.,* pp. 18-19

13. *Ibid.,* p. 54

14. Picasso's sheet metal and wire construction *Guitar* of 1912 (The Museum of Modern Art, New York) is a prime example of a Cubist realization of a work which is neither painting nor three-dimensional sculpture. This construction suggested countless possibilities to other artists.

and Kandinsky had left Russia because they believed in art for its own sake and not in the service of any other cause, such as the state. Tatlin, Rodchenko and Lissitzky continued their careers as artist-engineers with greater stress on the latter; they devoted themselves to the government in an effort to combine their artistic pursuits with the needs and demands of the state, an effort that proved futile in a system which was hostile to non-representational art.

Technology did not catch up with the ideas of Gabo and Pevsner until the late 30's and early 40's. Plastic, which allowed for greater delicacy and transparency, became available, and works like *Linear Construction in Space No. 1, 1950,*[15] resulted. In this piece and others like it, the importance of light has been increased to enhance the artist's manipulation of positive and negative

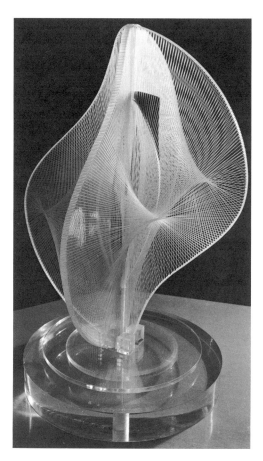

Naum Gabo
Linear Construction in Space No. 1, 1950

15. This piece is not included in the exhibition because it is too fragile to travel.

space. From the 30's on, Pevsner concentrated on exploring the inherent spatial contrasts of different metals. The Constructivists' handling and use of materials invariably differed from the Dadaists': the latter frequently relied on a juxtaposition of various materials or objects, often of a found or used nature which would result in an ironic statement. On the other hand, man-made or fabricated materials presented the greatest esthetic possibilities to the Constructivists who were encouraged to fully exploit the newest technological discoveries. As with Gabo, stretched lines and rods predominate in Pevsner's works whose organic and natural appearance belies their mathematical basis. In *Fresco, Fauna of the Ocean* (cat. no. 75) of 1944, the straight rods of copper and tin have been fused on the surface to create solid planes which turn and develop within a circular pattern. As a result, the surface appears to vibrate and dematerialize. Furthermore, the appearance of the material slowly changes because oxidation alters the original metal colors to create a luminous turquoise and gold hue. The strong rhythmic energy reiterates the actual motion of the universe, vividly recalling the Futurist "lines of force." Balla's *Fist of Boccioni; Lines of Force* (cat. no. 19) in form and title suggests most accurately a source of many Constructivist works; Balla's sculpture exemplifies a theoretical fusion of physical (the fist) and cosmological (lines of force) energy and tension.

Consistent with their advanced notions, Gabo and Pevsner stressed the importance of "a synthesis of the plastic arts: painting, sculpture and architecture...."[16]—again, a type of structural fusion. Lissitzky (cat. no. 61), however, envisioned his art as an even more total statement which integrated all the applied arts, especially typography and photography. He had been a pupil-disciple of Malevich, but was equally enthusiastic about Tatlin and Rodchenko's concern with the unity of art and the state. Like van Doesburg, his personality enabled him to bridge the gap between the two fundamentally opposite approaches. Van Doesburg (cat. no. 37) originally championed the pure and ideal esthetics of the *De Stijl* movement, and later embraced the theories and theatrics of Dada as well. With his wife, Nelly, and Schwitters, van Doesburg traveled throughout Holland presenting Dada lectures and performances. He wrote Dada poetry under the pseudonym of I.K. Bonset, only to be warned by his former *De Stijl* colleague Mondrian about an unknown writer whose ideas seemed extremely dangerous and anarchistic. Of course, this writer was van Doesburg himself, in his Dada guise! This assimilation of contrasting viewpoints does not point to a schizophrenic tendency in van Doesburg; on the contrary, it reveals his personal sense of the inherent similarities of both movements and the equal need of each to construct new realities.

All the artists discussed here were intent upon creating a total world view. Whether it is a Schwitters collage or an Arp sculpture, a Lissitzky Proun painting or a Pevsner construction—the intention of the artist was based on the profound need to construct a new vision in relation to the contemporary world. Without doubt, the Futurists were instrumental in furthering and expanding the highly influential Cubist breakthrough. Widening the scope of their art by introducing social and political elements and including allied media like photography, they affected the artists associated with Dada and the fantastic on the one hand and Constructivism and geometric abstraction on the other. The esthetic reverberations of Futurism are still felt today in such areas as kinetic and environmental art, as well as performances.

A particular emphasis on the collection has been the basis for this discussion. Alternate possibilities exist; different connections and conclusions may be drawn. The Winston/Malbin Collection offers the viewer, no matter what path is followed, a rewarding insight into twentieth-century art.

LINDA SHEARER

16. Quoted in *Gabo-Pevsner, op. cit.,* p. 57

Malbin living room , 1969

Umberto Boccioni in studio, c. 1913, with plaster of *Synthesis of Human Dynamism*, 1912 (destroyed)

Futurism Now

"Bisogna perdonare qualche sbaglio . . . all'uomo che tenta di volare"
"You must pardon the man who seeks to fly . . . if he makes some errors"

Boccioni to Barbantini

Boccioni's impassioned plea, made in 1911, is one of the many moving testimonies to the great struggle which he imposed upon himself in his brief and intense career. In retrospect Boccioni's outcry may also be viewed as a metaphorical appeal for a sympathetic and, more importantly, a balanced assessment of the Futurists' endeavors. For it seems that no twentieth-century creative effort has been subjected to such continuing, highly colored, hence misleading and often incorrect interpretation as Futurism. Such distortions were partly brought on by the Futurists themselves: their overambitiousness, swagger and exaggeration were intended to arouse, astound and offend, and could not but result in a vehement, partisan response. In addition, the movement's equivocal and complex connections with the rise and later triumph of Fascism have further clouded the evaluation of Futurism. And lastly, the very shape of the movement, its efforts to encompass all the arts and even establish a mode of life, has tended to confuse and discourage all but the most persistent of its students. However, the perspective imposed by time has also revealed some of the deeper reasons for the difficulties in comprehending and assessing this Italian contribution to modern art. Factors such as those mentioned above are relatively superficial. It is becoming increasingly apparent that Futurism was not only contradictory, but was more prophetic and daring than had been suspected. And, generally, the Italian movement, in all of its manifestations, emerges as one of the earliest and, above all, most inclusive and vocal expressions of the great creative and moral concerns of our century. These ingredients doubtless have given the Futurist message its continuing appeal.

Turning to some of the better known external aspects of the Italian movement, one notes, for example, that the Futurists' image of themselves as artists, their attitudes towards society and their methods differed markedly from those who preceded them and from most of their contemporaries. Rather than accepting and propagating the comfortable clichés about the artist as a disheveled but proud escapist loner, they were fashionably dressed and appeared easy-going; their projected image was that of energetic and powerful world leaders or industrialists. Quite resolutely they discarded for themselves and the public the nostalgic idea of the artist as a romantic anachronism, like the imaginary artisan of the past. Baldly, if somewhat suicidally, the Futurists faced the fact that in order to put their creative views across they had to employ the methods (and some of the attitudes) of the controlling sectors of society. Their brilliantly planned international and national exhibition, lecture and performance campaigns resemble Henry Ford shaping his empire. For it was with enterprises such as these that the Futurists had to compete for attention from a commodity and consumption-oriented public. Their aggressive and often trying methods were relieved and humanized by the group's youthful high-spirits, which turned all of their activities into hilarious, if irreverent, events. Beneath the din and dust of their uproar there appeared a firm optimism and courage. Italians called them *gli allegri futuristi* (the happy Futurists), for the mood of excitement and expectancy which they created was a welcome change from the pessimism and sensuous self-abandon of some of their elders.

Umberto Boccioni in studio, 1913.
Boccioni is standing to right behind his *Spiral Expansion of Muscles in Movement* (destroyed).
Seated are Giacomo Balla and Boccioni's mother.

Three of the Futurists during World War I, 1915

Futurism was given its public life and form in 1909 by the poet F. T. Marinetti (1876-1944), who was its leader and catalytic spirit. Quite possibly, Marinetti's most noteworthy contribution to culture, like that of his Russian contemporary Diaghilev, was the successful creation of a unified artistic ensemble, made up of disparate yet temporarily cooperating individuals. To extend the analogy further, it may be said that like Diaghilev's principal dancers, each of the Futurists placed his personal endeavors in the service of an all-encompassing vision and dedicated himself totally to its fulfillment. Yet Marinetti received as much as he gave. An extremely alert and perceptive impresario, he welcomed and thrived, as did the movement, on the lively exchange and collision of ideas within it. However, these differences which ultimately became irreconcilable, led in part to the collapse of the first phase of the movement around 1915.

Futurism achieved an esprit de corps that was both more intense and vocal than, for example, that of the French Impressionists or *Die Brücke* group of Dresden. These other artists had banded together for united strength in order to better pursue creative goals that ran counter to the dominant conventions. But the Italians, from the beginning, demanded a much greater discipline and militancy from themselves and from those they sought to reach. This was expressed in fierce exhortations such as Marinetti's proclamation in his celebrated Futurist Foundation Manifesto of 1909: "We shall sing the love of danger, the habit of energy and fearlessness." Such a mode of life, creative and otherwise, represented, above all, the Futurists' determination to combat the mental, moral and physical lethargy that seemed to have overcome mankind, partly as a result of the greater wealth and ease which the industrial age had brought about. The external complacency and comfort of human existence had reduced the arts to an agreeable, relaxing pastime for "rich and mature men with scornful minds and very bad digestion, which makes all mental effort impossible," in Marinetti's words.[1] The Futurists clearly recognized that the scope of art, as well as the conditions for its creation, had so narrowed as to threaten it with meaninglessness or annihilation. They were by no means the first to note this cultural crisis, in the making for over a century. But with the help of Schopenhauer, Nietzsche, Sorel, Whitman, Jarry and many others, they took the lead in many respects in diagnosing it afresh and in seeking a remedy. And in their fundamental efforts and their willingness to risk all for art, they provided fuel and guidelines for contemporary and subsequent quests for regeneration and liberation of the human spirit.

Today it seems obvious to assert that creation for the Futurists involved an intensely intimate awareness of and identification with the dynamic spirit and forces that the modern scientific and technological era had revealed. Yet what this implied in practice has still not been spelled out fully. What is clear, and cannot be stressed enough, is that it meant much more than "automobilism," as Wyndham Lewis bitingly characterized the Futurist doctrine in 1914. The realization that the mode of perception of modern life had been as drastically altered as life itself was a significant aspect of the Futurist esthetic; yet it implied more than this. Basically, Futurism stood for an extensive and unsparing questioning of the nature and place of art in the twentieth century, necessary if art were to survive and evolve as a profound human manifestation. The questioning begun by the Futurists aimed beyond the soul-searching of previous generations, which in their estimation had been far too limited. Marinetti's over-quoted slogan from the Foundation Manifesto that "a racing car . . . is more beautiful than the *Victory of Samothrace*" brutally points to the crux of the matter as he saw it: that the tension between the past and present, between dream and reality, or human will and failure, could in the twentieth century no longer be accommodated by the kinds of compromise that all speculative spirits effect in order to create.

It is significant that the *mise au point* of the modern artistic dilemma was posed not by a Frenchman but by an Italian (although a Francophile), and rapidly acted upon by a number of the most gifted and adventurous of his countrymen. Could it have been that such a bare revelation was more

1. *Manifesto dei drammaturghi,* broadsheet dated October 11, 1910, Poesia, Milan

Boccioni in studio, c. 1914, against *Materia*, 1912

readily achieved in Italy? For in the clear, unsparing light of this peninsula all human achievements, artistic, moral and other, dwindle in stature before the ubiquity of its bygone giants. The directness of the Futurists' protest, the extremes to which they went in communicating and fighting this malaise, can perhaps only be grasped fully within this local context. The fact that Italy then believed itself to be behind in cultural and socio-economic matters, and the widespread disillusionment in the aftermath of the *Risorgimento* may further have sharpened the Futurists' insight into the broader predicament of western civilization.

From the beginning, Futurism thus burdened itself with a moral charge similar in weight and urgency to that which fired the medieval artist of the eleventh and twelfth centuries. With analogous, near barbaric force the modern Italians attempted to expurgate the ready-made, meretricious and soothing alibis which filled men's minds and deflected them from the essential issues. And like their predecessors they emphasized that spiritual, hence creative survival could only be assured through war-like vigilance and combat, which Marinetti believed to be the heart of human existence. His exclamation of 1909 that "war is the world's only hygiene," therefore stands for more than a simple-minded, chauvinistic celebration of the actual thrills of battle. However, in his more adolescent, unreflective moments Marinetti was not unreceptive to these superficial sensations.

The widespread and seemingly distorted view that Futurist words preceded deeds should be discussed. This over-simplification has permitted an all too easy dismissal of Futurism as primarily a verbal program rather than an actual, self-contained and meaningful artistic phenomenon. And not surprisingly, such a view has supported the notion of an easy and direct transition from Futurism to Fascism, in which words were indeed one of the most profuse products. Futurism did, of course, burst forth with a seemingly endless number of manifestos, but its basic creative views were the result of prolonged gestation in the work of its guiding figures. But the Futurists' expository statements do raise the difficult and well-worn problem of the relationship of actual creation to its verbal justification. As the century passes and commentaries by artists multiply, providing a seeming permission, even invitation, to transpose one for the other, this problem becomes even more acute. Such curious and deliberate over-intellectualizations, an acerb comment on the creative anxiety of the present, are ultimately traceable to Futurism. This should not blind us to the fact that the Italians initially composed their verbal statements quite simply for purposes of publicity, public illumination, as well as personal clarification. The need to do this, as suggested earlier, was implied in their efforts to give the arts a central and dramatic place in human existence.

Futurism originated in a literary milieu with a principally literary point of view. Yet it may not be unjust to suggest that its most distinguished and, in a sense, most fulfilled early contributions were made in the visual arts. However, the Futurists' intrepid efforts to break down the borders between the different disciplines resulted in hybrids such as "free-word poetry," "free-word painting," "art of noises," kinetic, multi-material, colored, noise-making "plastic complexes," which, in their day, were radically novel. Hence in any evaluation one must make allowances for the cross-fertilization that, whether obvious or subtle, underlies most Futurist contributions.

What was most important in primarily determining the artistic direction of this closely knit group? Although not acknowledged at first, one of the most fundamental points of agreement among the painters and writers was their awareness of the double-edged thrust of photography and the moving picture as a powerful means of visual communication. The Futurists accepted these new media as direct artistic challenge and inspiration, although, at first, they denied such dependence. Their early detractors, however, had been quick to point out this influence. The Italians understood from the beginning that the survival of their own media was sharply threatened. The dual consequences—the threat and the inspiration—of photography had been recognized and responded to by artists ever since its invention in the second quarter of the nineteenth century. But the advent of the enormously appealing and popular moving picture seems to have heightened the competitive challenge of the mechanical eye. And Futurism, with its anti-traditional and dynamic esthetic was undoubtedly the first large-scale and consistently worked-out attempt to provide "artistic" counterparts to the mechanically achieved illusion of movement that the photographic lens had revealed. Almost predictably, in 1916 the first phase of Futurism, after considerable internal change, culminated in an effort to transform the "traditionless," esthetically innocent film into an all-embracing, multi-media form of expression. The film *Vita futurista* and the accompanying manifesto of *Futurist Cinematography* testify to the open acceptance of the camera by the movement.

Specific debts to the camera and its related discoveries are clearly discernible in early Futurist works and theory. It must be added that ideas pertaining to optical, psycho-physiological or philosophical aspects of perception almost simultaneously helped to stimulate, rationalize and dignify the Futurists' recourse to the camera. For example, the scientific principles underlying Neo-Impressionism—one of their chief technical points of departure—came to the Futurists' attention through some of its French exponents and apologists and through their Italian counterparts, the Divisionists. Or theories of empathy reached them in such diverse forms as those of Lipps, Berenson, Bergson, and through their socio-artistic elaboration in Romains' *Unanimisme*. Unquestionably, Bergson is an extremely important Futurist source, especially with regard to verbal justifications of their endeavors. For the French philosopher, probably more than any other thinker of the period, was able to translate contemporary spiritual yearnings into evocative metaphors. These provided attractive rubrics for many of the expressed or non-verbalized and often contradictory ideals of the time.

The Futurists' rejection of the conventions of time and space, the experimentation with both analytic and synthetic renditions of motion, and lastly, their quest for a powerful artistic analogue for the universal flux—Bergson's "duration" and Boccioni's "painting of states of mind"—can all, at least in part, be explained as outgrowths of the photographic/cinematic experience. Names famous in the history of photography, especially Marey and his chronophotography, are usually connected with the Futurists' more or less systematic studies of sequential motion, as found, for example, in Severini's *Study for "Portrait of Mme. M.S."* (cat. no. 99). In addition, the even more astounding early trick films with their flashbacks, montages and close-ups, or the X-ray photograph, are very close to the artists' search for an ultimately non-representational symbolic idiom.

All of these catalytic elements led to an early discovery by the Futurists that the static, confined art-object was insufficient for their purposes. From mid-1910, one finds pictorial allusions to and discussions, first, of an art of colored gases and, later, of colored lights which literally envelop the spectator. Talk of such liberated, abstract possibilities was in the air, as witnessed by such famous, roughly contemporary, theatrical projects as Kandinsky's *Der Gelbe Klang (The Yellow Sound)*, or Gordon Craig's vision of an actorless stage with dramatically lit and moving props. Very likely, the most complete and prophetic early realization of these ideas was accomplished by Balla in his decor of 1917 for Stravinsky's *Feu d'artifice*. This "dancerless ballet," commissioned by Diaghilev, demonstrated theatrically the Futurist desideratum of placing the spectator in the center of the work of art. By means of a time-controlled spatial interaction of sound, moving three-dimensional abstract colored forms and colored lights, which played on and off stage, Balla transformed the entire auditorium into a synesthetic ambience. Balla was the only one among the original Futurist artists able to carry on with the aims of the movement after the group had broken apart. By late 1916 its most forceful member, Boccioni, was dead, and Carrà and Severini had turned away from Futurism.

The Winston/Malbin collection, so sensitively and intelligently assembled, conveys a fine sense of the general course of Futurism and its aftermath. In so doing, it also reveals some of the difficulties that confront the modern artist, which, not unexpectedly, came newly into focus during the prime years of Futurism. These seem to point to an often unspoken awareness that the discovery and development of alternatives for the western tradition, outworn in their view, pose greater obstacles than anticipated. The technical and mechanical problems arising from the Futurists' wish to supersede the conventional, arrested representational likeness, as well as the isolated static art object were enormous, but not insurmountable. Early in the century, Balla's abstract decor, the work of the Constructivists and the *De Stijl* group variously fulfilled some of these requirements with great conviction and ingenuity. On the other hand, the force of past artistic civilization has proved to be a more stubborn problem, perhaps beyond resolution. The conscious or unconscious dialogue with this seemingly indestructible heritage, which had given human meaning and resonance to earlier creative efforts, has persisted to the present.

It is evident that the critical tension which characterizes the mature Futurism of Boccioni and of most of the other participants was brought to the surface by their contact with Cubism, which began in mid-1911. To Futurist eyes, Cubism as an artistic idiom and social phenomenon represented the kind of creative compromise which they had fiercely rejected as anachronistic; yet, as individuals and on purely artistic grounds, they desired and even envied it. For Cubism, unlike Futurism, was bred and sheltered in a nation with a prized modern tradition and supported by a few informed and wealthy apologists of the "new." Hence its purest masters, Picasso, Braque and Gris, were able to work within an austerely circumscribed artistic realm and to update radically some aspects of the classical heritage. Cubism thus remained proudly traditional and hermetic, deliberately sidestepping some of the artistic issues which the optimistic Italians faced.

The Futurists wished, above all, to communicate and to communicate with power. And Boccioni, whose work is as ingenuous as it is ardent, lays bare in his three sculptural masterworks, *Anti-Graceful, Development of a Bottle in Space, Unique Forms of Continuity in Space* (cat. nos. 28, 29, 30) some of the high ambitions and conflicts of Futurism. This extraordinarily gifted artist identified by natural inclination more closely with the ethos of Futurism than most of the other participants in the movement. Thus, quickly and dramatically, he gave substance to Marinetti's initial precepts, allowing the movement to expand and grow and survive artistically after his death.

On the most immediate level, Boccioni's three sculptures represent spirited attacks on the palatable academic standbys—the portrait, the still life and the monumental figure—with their usually banal conceits alluding to eternal attributes. On a more constructive plane, the sculptures, executed successively in 1912-13, are increasingly searching tests in three dimensions of the persistent interaction of objects with their environment and the mutual transformations that result. In this, they provide a brilliant adaptation and development of some of the analytic and synthetic procedures of Cubism. At the same time, they are also a partial answer to the problem posed by the Futurist belief that the flat surface of a painting had become insufficient for a forceful symbolic expression of the vital continuum. Yet Boccioni's use of a single material, rather than proceeding with his earlier multi-material assemblages, reflects his often-noted realization that he was seeking solutions for too many problems at once. He thus left it for Balla, his Russian contemporaries and their joint heirs to carry on along those lines.

One does not know if and how Boccioni would have wished to have his pieces cast. But the bronze versions by which they are now mostly known, give them a startlingly appropriate old-master look, while, at the same time, underlining their revolutionary quality. This dramatizes the struggle that seems to have been waged in the artist's mind in the course of creating them and which is symbolically communicated. The sculptures express Boccioni's—and by extension, man's—consuming desire to assert his momentary presence in the engulfing stream of change, seeking to shape it and himself to a harmonious concordance. The violent spiritual and material vicissitudes to which

Dr. and Mrs. Barnett Malbin in living room of the Malbin home

the subject, his mother, and sculptural form are subjected in this encounter, shown in *Anti-Graceful,* give way to the highly controlled and calculated, but still undecided contest of the *Bottle.* And finally, a triumphant breakthrough is achieved and proudly proclaimed in the weightless, soaring figure of *Unique Forms.* This metamorphosed multi-image, now motorcyclist-flyer, now flame and wave, possesses the complete formal ease appropriate to its statement. Boccioni has succeeded, as Apollinaire hoped the Cubists would, in "elevat[ing] the melody to a symphony."[2] Ironically, this breakthrough was accomplished with perhaps some unconscious and certainly grudging concessions to that derided paradigm of past beauty and dynamic action, the *Victory of Samothrace,* as has often been pointed out.[3] With it goes the tacit but increasingly pervasive admission, in Boccioni's work after late 1913, that art must draw on art. References to the uncircumventible presence of the classical past, filtered through Cézanne, appear with increasing frequency in his late paintings. Boccioni's acceptance of the seemingly unbreakable chain of tradition becomes tantamount to his recognition, verbalized only shortly before his death, that the wish to achieve an artistic regeneration was great enough a burden for one life.

Marinetti, more resilient and more thoroughly iconoclastic than Boccioni, never went so far as to admit these insights openly. But a similar awareness is implicit in his directives issued to the remaining Futurists during the War. He recommends that they simplify their work to make it comprehensible and fulfill propagandistic purposes. Similarly, Marinetti's growing involvement in the theatrical and cinematic activities of the movement bespeak, in part, his concession that the public and art cannot be served to the same extent at the same time. Yet the discoveries made in these areas, even if rudimentary, attest to the unflagging vitality of the Futurist impulse.

Whereas Cubism, with its narrow but deep commitments, had precipitated the artistic crisis of Futurism, the War pointed up the social one. Futurism, in keeping with its reforming aims, had from the beginning, pretended to a political role, and the actual and increasingly dominant politicizing of the movement that started in 1915, brought its fundamental dilemma to a head. Other idealistic European artistic endeavors experienced a similar trauma at the time. In desperation, some of the German Expressionists and Russian Constructivists, like the Futurists, linked their hopes for worldly fulfillment of their dreams to extremist revolutionary groups. In all instances these political bodies first exploited these artists, but once in power, sooner or later rejected them. For the underlying message of spiritual freedom that such artists brought to real politics threatened the self-propagation of those in power.

Marinetti's seemingly life-long friendship with Mussolini is as difficult to fathom as his acceptance in 1929 of membership in the Italian Academy. Did these acts mean, as is often said, that Marinetti travestied all that Futurism had stood for, and, worse still, that Futurism was one of the many roads to Fascism? In a sense the answer must, of course, be yes. But the condemnation of Futurism as a misguided enterprise does not necessarily follow. Rather it tragically suggests that Marinetti, the "St. John the Baptist of Futurism" in his blind and boundless zeal accepted the temporary death of Futurism in Fascism "much as Christianity was quenched by the Spanish Inquisition or charity by bishops."[4] This remark was made in 1938 by the English painter and ex-Futurist C.R.W. Nevinson. Yet Futurism lives so long as men dream and "keep alive the primal wonder and curiosity concerning the universe,"[5] as the keen American critic Christian Brinton had noted two decades earlier.

MARIANNE W. MARTIN

2. Guillaume Apollinaire, *Chroniques d'Art (1902-1918),* Gallimard, Paris, 1960, p. 217

3. See, for example, John Golding, *Boccioni's Unique Forms of Continuity in Space,* University of Newcastle-upon-Tyne, 1972, p. 26

4. C.R.W. Nevinson, *Paint and Prejudice,* Harcourt Brace, New York, 1938, pp. 89-90

5. Christian Brinton, *Impressions of the Art at the Panama-Pacific Exposition,* John Lane, New York, 1916, p. 26

Constantin Brancusi, Paris

Works in the Exhibition

PAINTINGS, SCULPTURE, WORKS ON PAPER

The listing is alphabetical by artist and chronological within individual artists. References to literature and exhibitions which are abbreviated are entered in full in the documentation section starting on page 230. At the end of every entry, the Winston/Malbin Collection number (W-00 or G-00) is noted. Height precedes width in all dimensions. The third dimension listed in sculpture is depth.

Josef Albers b. 1888

Born in Bottrop, Westphalia, Germany. 1913-20 studied art
in Berlin, Essen, Munich; subsequently at Bauhaus, Weimar.
1923 became professor at Bauhaus; moved with the school to
Dessau and developed *Vorkurs,* an introduction to design
based on the study of color, texture, form and line. 1933
upon closing of Bauhaus, moved to United States; headed art
department at Black Mountain College, North Carolina to
1949. 1949 beginning of series *Homage to the Square.* To
art school, Yale University, 1949; Chairman of Department
of Design 1950-58. Author of many books and articles.
Now retired from teaching career, works in New Haven.

1. JOSEF ALBERS

Study for "Mirage A." 1940
Oil on paper, 12 x 13½″
Unsigned

PROVENANCE:

The Pinacotheca Gallery, New York
Winston Collection, 1946

EXHIBITIONS:

Cranbrook, 1951, no. 1
University of Michigan, 1955, no. 1, p. 9
D.I.A., 1957-58, no. 2, p. 33, ill. p. 34
Indiana University, 1971, *Reflection*, no. 2, p. 31, ill. p. 31
D.I.A., 1972-73

REFERENCES:

Degand and Arp, *Aujourd'hui*, 1957, ill. p. 31
Read, Herbert, *A Concise History of Modern Painting,*
Praeger, New York, 1959, no. 113, p. 349, ill. p. 306 (hereafter cited as Read, *Modern Painting,* 1959)

G-125

Karel Appel b. 1921

Born in Amsterdam. 1940-1943 studied at Royal Academie
of Fine Arts, Amsterdam. 1946 first one-man exhibition
Beerenhuis, Groningen, Holland. 1948 founded Dutch
experimental artists group *Reflex,* with Constant and
Corneille, which became known as *Cobra* in Paris. 1950
settled in Paris. 1951 met critic Michel Tapié; began laying
colors on thickly. 1953-54 works included in important
international exhibitions; received UNESCO prize; first
United States one-man exhibit at Martha Jackson Gallery,
New York. 1960 first prize, Guggenheim International
Exhibition. Exhibition of sculptures, wall reliefs, paintings
1968-69 Centre National d'Art Contemporain, Paris;
Stedelijk Museum, Amsterdam; Kunsthalle, Basel; Palais
des Beaux—Arts, Brussels. 1972 major retrospective
organized by Musée d'Art Contemporain, Paris, toured
Canada. Lives in Auxerre, France.

2. KAREL APPEL

Head and Fish. 1954
Oil on canvas, 34¾ x 45¾″
l.r. " '54/K. Appel"

PROVENANCE:

the artist
Winston Collection, 1955 (through The Museum of
Modern Art, New York)

EXHIBITIONS:

The Museum of Modern Art, New York, May 10-August
7, 1955, *The New Decade: 22 European Painters and
Sculptors.* Travelled to The Minneapolis Institute of Arts,
September 21-October 30, 1955; Los Angeles County
Museum of Art, November 21, 1955-January 7, 1956; San
Francisco Museum of Art, February 2-March 15, 1956
D.I.A., 1957-58, no. 3, p. 33, ill. p. 34
D.I.A., March 8-April 7, 1963, *The Dutch Contribution to
The International Development of Art Since 1945*

REFERENCE:

The Detroit Free Press, March 3, 1963, ill.

W-142

Alexander Archipenko 1887-1964

Born in Kiev, Ukraine, Russia. 1902-05 studied art in Kiev, 1906-07 Moscow, 1908 Paris; considered himself self-taught. 1908 settled in Paris. 1912 executed first *Sculpto-Peintures* combining various materials and painted surfaces. Exhibited frequently in Paris Salons. Moved to New York 1923. 1924-27 invented *Archipentura,* kinetic paintings. In late 40's and 50's made electrically-lit plastic sculptures.

3. ALEXANDER ARCHIPENKO

Nude No. 1. c. 1912-13
Crayon on paper, 14 x 10½″
l.r. "Archipenko"

PROVENANCE:

Librairie Kundig, Geneva
Liebman Collection, New York
Parke-Bernet Galleries, New York
Winston Collection, 1955

EXHIBITIONS:

D.I.A., 1957-58, no. 4-a, p. 33. Did not travel
Indiana University, 1971, *Reflection,* no. 11, p. 33, ill. p. 36

REFERENCE:

Parke-Bernet Galleries, New York, 1955, *The Liebman Collection of Valuable Modern Paintings, Drawings, and Sculpture,* no. 25, p. 8.

G-201

4. ALEXANDER ARCHIPENKO

Nude No. 2. c. 1912-13
Crayon on paper, 17½ x 11″
l.r. "Archipenko"

PROVENANCE:

Librairie Kundig, Geneva
Liebman Collection, New York
Parke-Bernet Galleries, New York
Winston Collection, 1955

EXHIBITIONS:

D.I.A., 1957-58, no. 4-b, p. 33. Did not travel
Indiana University, 1971, *Reflection,* no. 10, p. 33

REFERENCE:

Parke-Bernet Galleries, New York, 1955, *The Liebman Collection of Valuable Modern Paintings, Drawings, and Sculpture,* no. 25, p. 8.

G-202

Jean Arp 1887-1966

Born in Strassburg, then part of German Alsace-Lorraine. Began career as a poet. 1904 published first poems; began to study art. Travelled to Germany, Paris. Exhibited 1912 *Blaue Reiter* exhibition, 1913 *Erster Deutscher Herbstsalon*. 1915 to Zurich. 1916-19 co-founder *Dada* movement. After 1916 made wood reliefs based on arrangements "according to the laws of chance." 1919-20 met Ernst and Schwitters. Participated in Dada and Surrealist movements during 1920's. 1922 married artist Sophie Tauber. 1926 settled in Meudon, France. 1930 first *papiers déchirés*. 1931-32 first sculpture in the round; member *Abstraction-Création*. 1940's many poems and woodcuts; 1946 first complete collection of poems published. 1949-50 first trip to United States. 1958 retrospective The Museum of Modern Art, New York. 1959 married Marguerite Hagenbach. 1963 Grand Prix National des Arts, Paris. 1950's and 60's monumental work. Died in Basel.

5. JEAN ARP

Head (Portrait of Tristan Tzara). c. 1920.
Ink and pencil on paper, 23⅝ x 17⅝"
l.l. "Arp"

PROVENANCE:

Tristan Tzara, Paris
Winston Collection, 1954

EXHIBITIONS:

D.I.A., 1957-58, no. 7, p. 35. Did not travel
Vassar College Art Gallery, Poughkeepsie, New York, May 19-June 10, 1961, *Centennial Loan Exhibition: Drawings and Watercolors from Alumnae and Their Families*, no. 113, ill. Travelled to Wildenstein & Co., New York, June 14-September 9, 1961. (hereafter cited as Vassar College, 1961, *Centennial Loan Exhibition*)
D.I.A., 1962, *French Drawings and Watercolors*
Indiana University, 1971, *Reflection*, no. 13, pp. 23, 33, ill. p. 23
D.I.A., 1972-73

REFERENCES:

Huyghe, René and Jean Rudel, *L'Art et le monde moderne: Volume I, 1880-1920*, Librairie Larousse, Paris, 1969, no. 1148, ill. p. 367. (hereafter cited as Larousse, 1969)
D.K., "Modern Masters in Groups," *The Milwaukee Journal*, April 11, 1971, part 5, p. 6, ill.

G-191

Like the two other Arp drawings—both titled *Abstract Form*, c. 1922—this one is an automatic drawing. It was not originally intended as a portrait of Tristan Tzara, although Lydia Malbin felt it looked enough like him to be named for him.

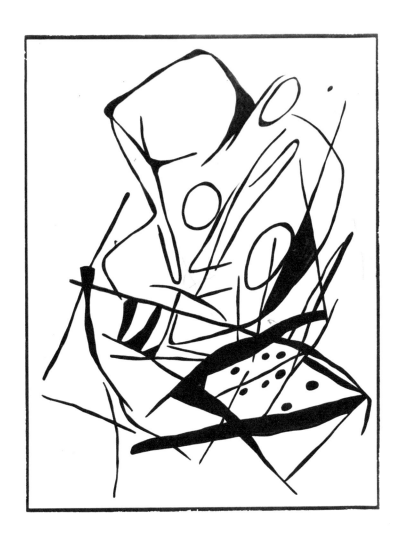

6. JEAN ARP

Abstract Form I. c. 1922
Ink on paper, 10 x 8″
l.r. "ARP"

PROVENANCE:

Tristan Tzara, Paris
Winston Collection, 1954

EXHIBITION:

D.I.A., 1957-58, p. 79. Did not travel

REFERENCE:

Indiana University, 1971, *Reflection,* no. 14, pp. 17, 34, ill.
p. 16

G-181

7. JEAN ARP

Abstract Form II. c. 1922
Ink on paper, 10 x 8″
l.r. "ARP"

PROVENANCE:

Tristan Tzara, Paris
Winston Collection, 1954

EXHIBITION:

D.I.A., 1957-58, p. 79. Did not travel

REFERENCE:

Indiana University, 1971, *Reflection*, no. 15, pp. 17, 34, ill.
p. 37

G-182

8. JEAN ARP

Bird Forms. 1922
Wood, 27½ x 9⅞ x 2¼″
Unsigned

PROVENANCE:

Walter P. Chrysler, Jr.
The Pinacotheca Gallery, New York
Winston Collection, 1950

EXHIBITIONS:

Cranbrook, 1951, no. 86, ill.
University of Michigan, 1955, no. 3, p. 9
D.I.A., 1957-58, no. 6, p. 35. Did not travel

W-140

9. JEAN ARP

Lunar Armor (Cuirasse lunaire). 1938
Granite, 12⅝ x 14⅝″
Unsigned

PROVENANCE:

the artist, Basel
Winston Collection, 1956

EXHIBITIONS:

Kunsthalle, Bern, April 7-May 6, 1956. *Hans Arp und Kurt Schwitters,* no. 7
D.I.A., 1957-58, no. 8, p. 35, ill. p. 28
The Museum of Modern Art, New York, October 8-November 30, 1958, *Jean Arp, Retrospective,* no. 77, p. 122, ill. p. 70
D.I.A., 1972-73

REFERENCES:

Arp, Jean, *On My Way: Poetry and Essays, 1912-1947,* Wittenborn, New York, 1948, pl. 29-a,b
Degand and Arp, *Aujourd'hui,* 1957, ill. p. 30
Giedion-Welcker, Carola, *Jean Arp,* New York, 1957, no. 50, p. 109
"The Winston Collection on Tour," *Arts,* ill. p. 35
Vassar Alumnae Magazine, 1958, ill. p. 11
Baro, *Art in America,* 1967, ill. p. 76
Baro, *The Collector in America,* 1971, p. 182

W-139

Upon seeing this work at the joint *Arp-Schwitters* exhibition in Bern in 1956, the Winstons were most anxious to count it among the other objects in their rapidly growing collection. After inquiring about the piece, they found that it belonged to the artist and was not for sale. The sculpture moved them so much however that they telephoned Arp and subsequently went to visit him and Marguerite Hagenbach in Basel. By the end of the visit, they had acquired *Lunar Armor,* having also formed the basis of what was to be a long and deep friendship with the artist and his future wife. According to Marguerite Hagenbach-Arp, this sculpture of her husband's is "a unique original, directly carved in pink limestone [sic] by Jean Arp." (quoted and translated from a letter in French to Lydia Winston Malbin, October 15, 1968.) It is one of the few pieces on which he actually worked himself and which was one of his "anonymous stones."

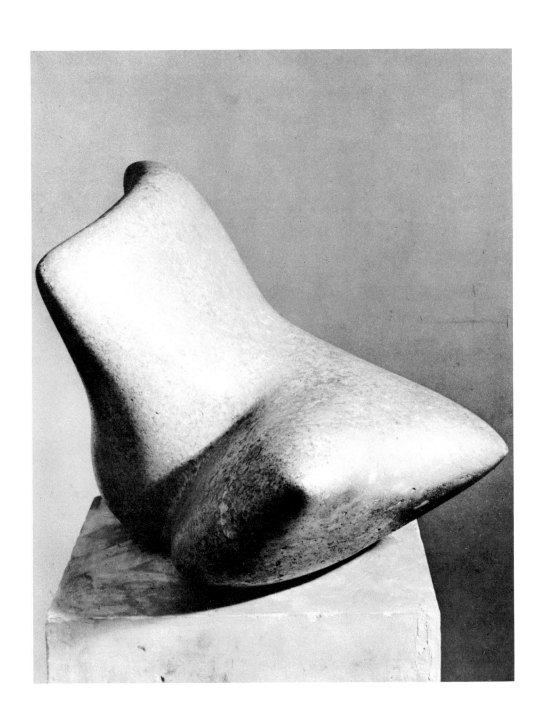

10. JEAN ARP

Dream Column; The School Boy (Colonne de rêve; L'Ecolier). 1938;1958
Limestone and bronze
Two sections: 20¼ x 8¼ x 3⅞″ top; 24 x 7⅞ x 7⅞″ bottom; 42½″ total height
Unsigned

PROVENANCE:

the artist, Meudon
Winston Collection, 1958

EXHIBITION:

D.I.A., 1972-73

REFERENCE:

Trier, Eduard, *Jean Arp, Sculpture—His Last Ten Years,* Abrams, New York, 1968, no. 172, p. 109, ill. p. 108

W-141

The upper portion dates from 1938, whereas the lower was made in 1958. The artist combined the two parts to make a single sculpture.

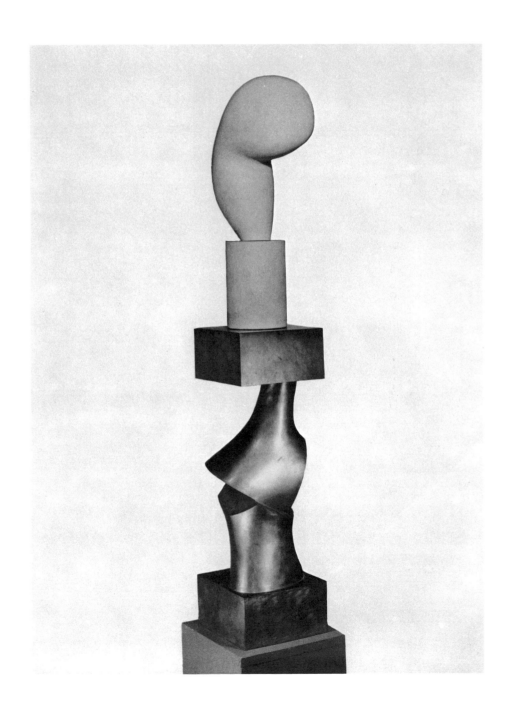

Giacomo Balla 1871-1958

Born in Turin. Studied art evenings in Turin. 1895 to Rome which remained center of his activity; worked as illustrator, caricaturist, portrait painter. 1900-01 in Paris for 7 months. Upon return to Rome met Boccioni, Severini, Sironi; taught them Divisionist technique. Signed later editions of two Futurist painting manifestos, 1910; however did not participate importantly in Futurist activities until 1913. Was painter, sculptor, theater and interior designer and playwright. Sustained Futurist impetus longer than other early participants; became leader of later phases of movement. Middle 1930's returned to more figurative style in somewhat Impressionist manner.

11. GIACOMO BALLA

Work (Il Lavoro). 1902

Oil on canvas, 68 x 48½″

l.l. "BALLA 1902"; l.r. "BALLA"; on reverse " 'Lavoro' di Giacomo Balla, 1902, Roma"

PROVENANCE:

the artist
Umberto Spironello, Rome
Luce and Elica Balla, Rome, 1952
Winston Collection, 1959

EXHIBITIONS:

Società Amatori e Cultori, Rome, 1904, *LXXVI Esposizione Internazionale di Belle Arti*, no. 1057
XXVI Biennale, Venice, June 14-October 19, 1952, no. 50, p. 396
Palazzo Reale, Milan, April 30-June 26, 1960, *Arte italiana del XX secolo da collezioni americane*, no. 8, p. 192, ill. p. 24. Travelled to Galleria Nazionale d'Arte Moderna, Rome, July 6-September 18, 1960. Special New York showing at Santini Brothers Warehouse, October 24 and 26, 1960 (hereafter cited as Milan, 1960, *Arte italiana*)
The Museum of Modern Art, New York, May 31-September 5, 1961, *Futurism*, no. 1, pp. 19-20, 141, ill. p. 18. Travelled to The Detroit Institute of Arts, October 18-December 19, 1961; Los Angeles County Museum, January 14-February 19, 1962 (hereafter cited as Museum of Modern Art, 1961, *Futurism*)

REFERENCES:

Roux, O., "La LXXIV Esposizione Internazionale di Belle Arti a Roma," *Natura e Arte*, vol. 26, 1903-04, p. 159
Bertolucci, Attilio, "La casa del futurista," *L'Illustrazione italiana*, vol. 85, no. 1, January 1958, ill. p. 61
"Italian Art of the 20th Century from American Collections," *Art International*, vol. IV, no. 5, May 25, 1960, ill. p. 21
Gambillo, Maria Drudi and Teresa Fiori, *Archivi del futurismo*, 1962, De Luca, Rome, vol. 2, no. 8, p. 151, ill. p. 67 (hereafter cited as *Archivi del futurismo*)
Crispolti, Enrico, "Situazione e percorso di Balla," Galleria Civica d'Arte Moderna, *Giacomo Balla*, 1963, p. 6
Ballo, Guido, *Boccioni*, Il Saggiatore, Milan, 1964, no. 58, ill. p. 67 (hereafter cited as Ballo, *Boccioni*, 1964)
Barricelli, Anna, *Balla*, De Luca, Rome, 1967, pl. 8
Bellonzi, Fortunato, *Il divisionismo nella pittura italiana*, Fabbri, Milan, 1967, ill. p. 73
Calvesi, Maurizio, "Penetrazione e magia nella pittura di Balla," *L'Arte moderna*, vol. v, no. 40, 1967, ill. p. 153
Fagiolo dell'Arco, Maurizio, "Boccioni, Beyond Painting," *Art International*, vol. XI, no. 1, January 20, 1967, p. 17
Francoeur, *Chicago Mid-West Art*, 1967, ill. p. 8
Fagiolo dell'Arco, Maurizio, *Balla pre-futurista*, Bulzoni, Rome, 1968, no. 35, ill. pp. 18, 41 (hereafter cited as Fagiolo, *Balla*, 1968)
Fiori, Teresa, *Archivi del divisionismo*, Officina, Rome, 1968, vol. 2, no. 1716, p. 139, ill. pl. 349 (hereafter cited as *Archivi del divisionismo*)
Martin, Marianne W., *Futurist Art and Theory, 1909-1915*, Clarendon Press, Oxford, 1968, p. 74, pl. 35 (hereafter cited as Martin, 1968)
Baro, *The Collector in America*, 1971, ill. p. 181
Galleria Nazionale d'Arte Moderna, Rome. December 23, 1971-February 27, 1972, *Giacomo Balla*, "Documenti fotografici," ill., n.p.

W-13

The painting shows Balla's mastery of Italian Divisionism as well as his fascination with the effects of nocturnal illumination. His concern with social questions is suggested here and in a number of other pre-Futurist works.

12. GIACOMO BALLA

Spring Buds (Germogli primaverili). c. 1906
Oil on canvas, 19¼ x 29¼″
l.l. "BALLA"; l.r. "BALLA"

PROVENANCE:

Luce Balla, Rome
Winston Collection, 1960

EXHIBITIONS:

VIII Quadriennale, Rome, 1959-60
XXX Biennale, Venice, June 18-October 16, 1960, no. 4,
p. 13

REFERENCES:

Ballo, *Boccioni,* 1964, no. 66, ill. p. 71
Archivi del divisionismo, vol. 2, no. 1792, p. 144, pl. 364
Fagiolo, *Balla,* 1968, no. 85, ill. pp. 25, 46

W-38

Balla has depicted a favorite early motif: the view from his
Roman studio in via Parioli (now via Paisiello) onto the row
of trees, shown below, which divided his yard from the
adjoining meadow of the Villa Borghese that fills most of the
canvas. The mysterious and dramatic shadow on the left
may have been cast by a wall.

13. GIACOMO BALLA

The Stairway of Farewells (Gli addii scala; Salutando).

c. 1908

Oil on canvas, 40¾ x 41″

l.r. "BALLA"

PROVENANCE:

the artist
Benedetta Marinetti, Rome
Winston Collection, 1958

EXHIBITIONS:

Società di Amatori e Cultori, Rome, 1910, *LXXX Exposizione Internazionale di Belle Arti,* no. 194, Tav. VI
Milan, 1960, *Arte italiana,* no. 9, p. 192, ill. frontispiece
Museum of Modern Art, 1961, *Futurism,* no. 3, p. 141, ill. p. 15
D.I.A., 1972-73

REFERENCES:

Colasanti, Arduino, "L'Esposizione internazionale d'arte in Roma," *Emporium,* vol. XXXI, no. 185, May 1910, p. 384
Apollonio, Umbro, "Il cinema tra spettacolo e arte figurativa," *La Biennale di Venezia,* no. 4, April 1951, ill. p. 41
Lucas, John, "Rome — Italian art from American Collections . . . the journalists draw a moral," *Arts,* vol. 34, no. 10, September 1960, ill. p. 19
Archivi del futurismo, vol. 2, no. 13, p. 152, ill. p. 69
Winston, *Aujourd'hui,* 1962, ill. p. 7
Carrieri, Raffaele, *Futurism,* Milione, Milan, 1963, pl. 18
Taylor, *Collections,* 1963, p. 302
Crispolti, Enrico, "Situazione e percorso di Balla," Galleria Civica d'Arte Moderna, Turin, *Giacomo Balla,* 1963, p. 15
Artist, Jr., vol. 5, no. 3, January 1964, ill. on cover
Stelzer, Otto, *Kunst und Photographie,* Piper, Munich, 1966, p. 122, pl. 118
Baro, *Art in America,* 1967, ill. p. 73
Barricelli, Anna, *Balla,* de Luca, Rome, 1967, pl. 24
Calvesi, Maurizio, "Penetrazione e magia nella pittura di Balla," *L'Arte moderna,* vol. V, no. 40, 1967, ill. p. 153
Archivi del divisionismo, vol. 2, no. 1790, p. 145, pl. 364
Fagiolo, *Balla,* 1968, no. 94, ill. pp. 26, 46
Martin, 1968, pp. 75-76, pl. 37
Miesel, *The Connoisseur,* 1968, fig. 7, ill. p. 262
Scharf, Aaron, *Art and Photography,* Lane, London, 1968, p. 289
Larousse, 1969, no. 1089, ill. p. 350
Baro, *The Collector in America,* 1971, ill. p. 181
Galleria Nazionale d'Arte Moderna, Rome, 1972, *Giacomo Balla,* "Documenti fotografici," ill., n.p.

W-17

This finely organized canvas anticipates some important
artistic desiderata of Futurism. Its hazardous and uncustom-
ary angle of vision like a vortex draws the spectator into the
depths of the picture. Balla's novel viewpoint as well as his
exploration of the dynamic potential of lines and shapes
were suggested at least in part by photographic experiments.
Thus the compelling image of the continuum of motion
created by the spiralling steps is an imaginative analogue
to the abstract oscillation patterns which Etienne-Jules
Marey derived from his chronophotographic images of
moving objects. Such abstract schemata were points of
departure not only for Balla's Futurist representation of
velocity, but also for works such as Boccioni's *Unique Forms
of Continuity in Space*.

14. GIACOMO BALLA

Study related to "Abstract Velocity"; Study for "Materiality of Lights + Speed." c. 1913

Gouache on paper, 11¾ x 17″

l.l. "FUTUR BALLA"

PROVENANCE:

Rose Fried, New York
Winston Collection, 1954

EXHIBITIONS:

Rose Fried Gallery, New York, January 25-February 26, 1954, *The Futurists: Balla, Severini, 1912-18*, no. 10
University of Michigan, 1955, no. 4, p. 9
D.I.A., 1957-58, no. 12, p. 35, ill. p. 36
The Museum of Modern Art, New York, November 25, 1968-February 9, 1969, *The Machine: As Seen at the End of the Mechanical Age*, ill. p. 56. Travelled to The University of St. Thomas, Houston, March 25-May 18, 1969; The San Francisco Museum of Art, June 23-August 24, 1969 (hereafter cited as Museum of Modern Art, *The Machine*, 1968-69)
D.I.A., 1972-73

REFERENCES:

Archivi del futurismo, vol. 2, no. 69, p. 154, ill. p. 82
Francoeur, *Chicago Mid-West Art,* 1967, ill. p. 9
Hamilton, George Heard, *Painting and Sculpture in Europe, 1880-1940,* Penguin, Baltimore, 1967, pl. 109B, pp. 182-83
Dorazio, Virgina Dortch, *Giacomo Balla: An Album of His Life and Work,* Wittenborn, New York, 1970, no. 114, ill., n.p. (hereafter cited as Dorazio, *Balla,* 1970)

W-31

In 1915 Balla declared that he had executed "more than twenty paintings" in which he "stud[ied] the speed of automobiles, and in so doing discovered the laws and essential force-lines of speed." He may well have counted this gouache among the group, four of which were illustrated in Boccioni's *Pittura scultura futuriste,* published in 1914. Two of these are entitled respectively, *Materiality of Lights + Speed* and *Abstract Velocity,* and this picture seems to be a close variant of the latter. Its terse abstraction provides a lucid ideogram of the interaction of speed, sound, light and dust, attesting to Balla's mastery of this paradigmatic Futurist subject.

15. GIACOMO BALLA

Iridescent Interpenetration (Compenetrazione iridescente).

Oil on canvas, 39⅛ x 23″

l.l. vertically "BALLA 1912"; on reverse "Compenetrazione
Iridescente/G. Balla"

PROVENANCE:

Luce Balla, Rome
Winston Collection, 1960

EXHIBITIONS:

Galleria Origine, Rome, April 1950, *Omaggio a G. Balla
futurista,* no. 18
Amici della Francia, Milan, November 10-December 2,
1951, *Giacomo Balla,* no. 6
Galleria Selecta, Milan, April 27-May 11, 1956, *Balla,
Opere scelte del periodo futurista*
Galerie Cahiers d'Art, Paris, April 12-May 11, 1957,
Giacomo Balla, no. 1
Palazzo Barberini, Rome, Spring 1959, *Il futurismo,* no. 51,
p. 61
XXX Biennale, Venice, June 18-October 16, 1960, no. 5,
p. 13
Museum of Modern Art, 1961, *Futurism,* no. 7, p. 141, ill.
p. 62
D.I.A., 1972-73

REFERENCES:

Colla, Ettore, "Pittura e scultura astratta di G. Balla," *Arti
visive,* September-October, 1952, ill., n. p.
Winston, *Aujourd'hui,* 1962, ill. p.8
Taylor, *Collections,* 1963, ill. p. 297
Galleria Civica d'Arte Moderna, Turin, 1963, *Giacomo
Balla,* p. 58
Calvesi, Maurizio, "Penetrazione e magia nella pittura di
Balla," *L'Arte moderna,* vol. V, no. 40, 1967, ill. p. 132
Rickey, George, *Constructivism: Origins and Evolution,*
Braziller, New York, 1967, p. 14, fig. 12, p. 15
Fagiolo dell'Arco, Maurizio, *Le "Compenetrazioni
Iridescenti,"* Bulzoni, Rome, 1968, no. 1, p. 43
Martin, 1968, pl. 172, pp. 176-77
Fagiolo dell'Arco, Maurizio, "Futur-BALLA," *Metro,*
no. 13, New Series, 1968, ill. no. 12, p. 61
Huyghe, René, *L'Impressionnisme,* Réalités-Hachette, Paris,
1971, p. 317, ill. p. 275
Apollonio, Umbro, ed. *Futurist Manifestos,* Viking, New
York, 1972, pl. 64
Fagiolo dell'Arco, Maurizio, "The Futurist Construction of
the Universe," *Italy: The New Domestic Landscape:
Achievements and Problems of Italian Design,* The Museum
of Modern Art, New York, 1972, p. 296
Rye, Jane, *Futurism,* Studio Vista, London, 1972, ill. p. 69

W-16

Balla's abstract, analytical studies of color date from a trip
to Düsseldorf during the winter of 1912. There he began a
series of small watercolors in which contrasting or more
closely related colors are arranged in patterns made up of
variously shaped triangles or segmented circles. At present
it is not known when Balla began to consider these abstract
studies as the basis for self-sufficient paintings such as the
splendid example in the Winston/Malbin Collection. The
first oil versions of this theme seem to have been executed
for decorative purposes from c. 1913 onward. Balla appears
not to have dared or cared to exhibit these significant
experiments until the 1950's when the evolution of abstract
art was newly reconsidered.

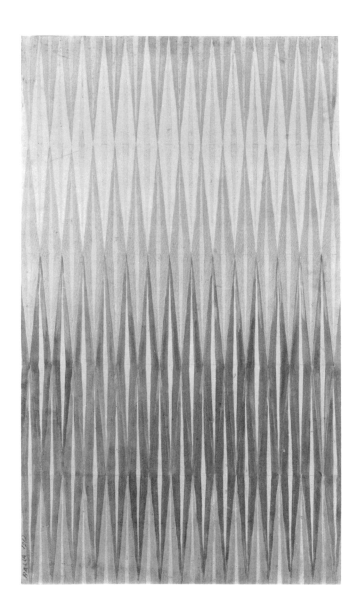

16. GIACOMO BALLA

Goldfish (Soleil au couchant poisson rouge-mer). c. 1914

Pastel on paper, 9¼ x 14¼"

Unsigned

PROVENANCE:

the artist
Benedetta Marinetti, Rome
Winston Collection, 1958

W-33

Balla presented this drawing to Madame Marinetti when
she was working in his studio, probably during 1914. It is
evidently related to Balla's numerous studies of velocity that
occupied him from 1913 onward. Compare, for example,
nos. 137, 139, ill. p. 97, *Archivi del futurismo,* vol. 2.

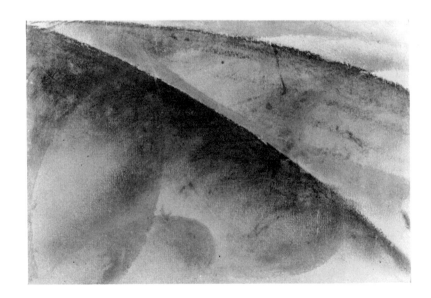

17. GIACOMO BALLA

Study for "Mercury Passing before the Sun." 1914
Gouache on paper, 25¾ x 19¾"
l.l. "FUTUR BALLA 1914"; on reverse "STUDIO PER IL—
MERCURIO CHE PASSA/DAVANTI AL SOLE/NEL
TELESCOPIO"

PROVENANCE:

the artist
Benedetta Marinetti, Rome
Winston Collection, 1954

EXHIBITIONS:

University of Michigan, 1955, no. 6, p. 9
D.I.A., 1957-58, no. 14, p. 35, ill. p. 36
The Baltimore Museum of Art, October 6-November 15,
1964, *1914: An Exhibition of Paintings, Drawings and
Sculpture,* no. 5, p. 82, ill. p. 76

REFERENCES:

Archivi del futurismo, vol. 2, no. 138, p. 158, ill. p. 97
Baro, *The Collector in America,* 1971, p. 182

W-25

This is one of several studies related to two larger versions of
the subject: one is in the collection of Dr. Gianni Mattioli,
Milan, the other in the Museum des 20. Jahrhunderts,
Vienna. Very possibly the partial eclipse of the sun of
November 7th, 1914, provided the impetus for this series.
Verso:
Pencil drawing of abstract forms similar to those used in the
series of *Interventionist Demonstrations (Dimostrazioni
interventiste)* of c. 1915. Inscription in pencil: "Via Paisiello
ORE 9 domani".

18. GIACOMO BALLA

Vortex + Line of Velocity (Vortice + linea di velocità;
Vortice) c. 1914-15
Pencil on paper, 16¾ x 25″
l.l. "FUTUR BALLA"

PROVENANCE:

Luce Balla, Rome
Winston Collection, 1960

EXHIBITIONS:

The Solomon R. Guggenheim Museum, New York, November 6, 1963-January 5, 1964, *20th Century Master Drawings,* no. 3. Travelled to University Gallery, University of Minnesota, Minneapolis, February 3-March 15, 1964; The Fogg Art Museum, Cambridge, April 6-May 24, 1964 (hereafter cited as Guggenheim, 1963-64, *20th Century Drawings*) D.I.A., 1972-73

REFERENCE:

Archivi del futurismo, vol. 2, no. 109, p. 157, ill. p. 92

G-176

19. GIACOMO BALLA

Fist of Boccioni; Force-Lines of the Fist of Boccioni (Pugno di Boccioni; Linee forze del pugno di Boccioni)
Plastic complex *(complesso plastico):* cardboard, wood and paint, 33 x 31 x 12½″
Unsigned

PROVENANCE:

Luce Balla, Rome
Winston Collection, 1959

EXHIBITIONS:

Museum of Modern Art, 1961, *Futurism,* no. 18, p. 142, ill. p. 117
D.I.A., 1972-73

REFERENCES:

Marchi, Virgilio, "Studio futurista di Balla," *Il Futurismo,* vol. I, no. 4, October 2, 1932, ill. p. 14
Bertolucci, Attilio, "La casa del futurista," *L'Illustrazione Italiana,* vol. 85, no. 1, January 1958, ill. p. 59
Calvesi, Maurizio, "Il futurismo e l'avanguardia europea," *La Biennale di Venezia,* vol. IX, nos. 36-37, December 1959, ill. p. 30
Pearlstein, Philip, "Futurism and Some Other Corrupt Forms," *Art News,* vol. 60, no. 4, Summer 1961, ill. p. 33
Archivi del futurismo, vol. 2, no. 224, p. 165, ill. p. 116
Galleria Civica d'Arte Moderna, Turin, 1963, *Giacomo Balla,* p. 108
Taylor, *Collections,* 1963, pl. 303
Read, Herbert, *A Concise History of Modern Sculpture,* Praeger, New York, 1964, no. 123, pp. 134, 288, ill. p. 124 (hereafter cited as Read, *Modern Sculpture,* 1964)
Baro, *Art in America,* 1967, ill. p. 76
Calvesi, Maurizio, "Penetrazione e magia nella pittura di Balla," *L'Arte moderna,* vol. V. no. 40, 1967, ill. p. 142
Fagiolo dell'Arco, Maurizio, *Omaggio a Balla,* Bulzoni, Rome, 1967, p. 47
Crispolti, Enrico, "Balla scultore," *Arte illustrata,* no. 2, February 1968, ill. p. 21
Fagiolo dell'Arco, Maurizio, *Balla: Ricostruzione futurista dell'universo,* Bulzoni, Rome, 1968, ill. no. 39, pp. 29, 77
Barilli, Renato, *La scultura del novecento,* Fabbri, Milan, 1968, pl. 34, p. 53
Dorazio, *Balla,* 1970, ills. nos. 159, 182, 191
Baro, *The Collector in America,* 1971, ill. p. 182
Galleria Nazionale d'Arte Moderna, Rome, December 23, 1971-February 27, 1972, *Giacomo Balla,* p. 167
Rye, Jane, *Futurism,* Studio Vista, London, 1972, ill. p. 53
Musée d'Art Moderne de la Ville de Paris, May 24-July 2, 1972, *Balla,* p. 150

W-14

A related graphic motif of *Boccioni's Fist* appeared on the front page of *Italia Futurista* of August 25th, 1916, which was dedicated to Boccioni who had died eight days earlier. This dynamic design may originally have been intended as a letterhead for the Futurist movement, and was used as such subsequently. It may have been conceived in 1915. The translation of the motif into three dimensions is consonant with the notion of "plastic complexes" as explained in Balla and Depero's manifesto *The Futurist Reconstruction of the Universe* of March 1915. The sculpture illustrated there (now lost), as well as Balla's set for Diaghilev's 1917 production of *Feu d'artifice,* made up of moving, abstract colored complexes, suggest that *Boccioni's Fist* may well have been executed during these years.

20. GIACOMO BALLA

Crowd and Landscape (Follo + Paesaggio; Paesaggio Folle Patriottiche). 1915?
Collage on paper, 60 x 26¼"
l.c. "BALLA FUTURISTA/1915"

PROVENANCE:

the artist
Benedetta Marinetti, Rome
Winston Collection, 1958

EXHIBITIONS:

Museum of Modern Art, 1961, *Futurism*, no. 17, p. 142
D.I.A., 1969, *Friends of Modern Art*, no. 23

REFERENCES:

Archivi del futurismo, vol. 2, no. 230, p. 165, ill. p. 117
Wescher, Herta, *Collage,* Abrams, New York, 1968, pl. 52, p. 403

W-21

Balla created this collage expressly for Marinetti to cover the mirror of his wardrobe because its reflections bothered the Futurist leader, who was ill at the time. Two other versions of this collage exist. The flat figure-eight has recently been interpreted as the emblem of the House of Savoy, the ruling Italian dynasty, thus representing a possible allusion to the vehement debate that raged in 1915 between the pro-intervention king and the anti-intervention government. On stylistic grounds, however, a date of c. 1918 would seem to be indicated; this is supported by the fact that Marinetti, who was injured at the front in 1917, was still convalescing in 1918.

21. GIACOMO BALLA

Futurist Necktie (Cravatta futurista). c. 1916
Watercolor, gouache and pencil on paper, 5 x 6⅛″
u.c. "No. 10 CRAVATTA FUTURISTA/ BALLA"

PROVENANCE:

Rose Fried Gallery, New York
Winston Collection, 1954

REFERENCE:

Dorazio, *Balla,* 1970, no. 195. Balla shown wearing one of
his neckties, 1925

W-236

Balla frequently wore Futurist outfits, as described in his
manifesto *Anti-neutral Clothing* (cat. no. 242), and his ties
especially caused sensations. Later accounts, perhaps somewhat embroidered, include Marinetti's story of Balla's
painted and sugared metal ties. And the architect Virgilio
Marchi recalls that the technical failures of the 1917
premiere of Balla's set for *Feu d'artifice* were counteracted
by the artist's appearance on stage with a tie that had
blinking lights.

22. GIACOMO BALLA

Path of a Gunshot (Colpo di fucile). c. 1918

Oil on canvas, 14¼ x 17¾″

l.l. "BALLA FUTURISTA"

PROVENANCE:

Il Milione, Galleria d'Arte Moderna, Milan
Winston Collection, 1954

EXHIBITION:

D.I.A., 1957-58, no. 11, ill. p. 35. Did not travel

REFERENCE:

Mellquist, *XXᵉ Siècle,* 1958, ill., n.p.

W-27

This is a pictorial representation of a noise perceived at great velocity. In October 1918, Balla exhibited a number of works with the title *Colpo di fucile domenicale (Path of a Sunday Gunshot)* at the Casa d'Arte Bragaglia, Rome, but it is difficult to ascertain whether this painting was included. Very possibly Balla alludes in this series to the revolutionary political activities of the Futurists at the time.

23. GIACOMO BALLA

The Injection of Futurism (Iniezione di futurismo). c. 1918
Oil on canvas, 31¾ x 45¼"
l.r. "INIEZIONE DI FUTURISMO/ BALLA/ FUTURISTA"
(Frame made and painted by the artist)

PROVENANCE:

the artist
Benedetta Marinetti, Rome
Winston Collection, 1954

EXHIBITIONS:

III Biennale, Rome, 1925, no. 11
V Quadriennale, Rome, 1948, no. 4, ill. p. 37
Galleria Origine, Rome, April 1951, *Omaggio a G. Balla futurista,* no. 1
University of Michigan, 1955, no. 5, ill. p. 17
D.I.A., 1957-58, no. 13, p. 35, ill. p. 37
Museum of Modern Art, 1961, *Futurism,* no. 20, p. 142, ill. p. 16
D.I.A., 1972-73

REFERENCES:

Cahiers d'Art, vol. XXV, no. 1, 1950, ill. p. 67
Saarinen, *Art News,* 1957, fig. 2, p. 65, ill. p. 33
Mellquist, *XXᵉ Siècle,* 1958, ill., n.p.
Ashton, Dore, "L'Exposition du Futurisme à New York," *XXᵉ Siècle,* Nouvelle Série, no. 17 (Noël) 1961, "Supplement—Chroniques du jour," ill. p. 149
Archivi del futurismo, vol. 2, no. 324, p. 171, ill. p. 134
Carrieri, Raffaele, *Futurism,* Milione, Milan, 1963, pl. 88
Galleria Civica d'Arte Moderna, Turin, 1963, *Giacomo Balla,* p. 82
Taylor, *Collections,* 1963, p. 294, ill. p. 303
Baro, *Art in America,* 1967, ill. p. 77
Calvesi, Maurizio, "Penetrazione e magia nella pittura di Balla," *L'Arte moderna,* vol. V, no. 40, 1967, ill. p. 134
Miesel, *The Connoisseur,* 1968, fig. 2, ill. p. 260

W-23

The vitalizing effect of Futurism with its explosive and gay atmosphere is suggested in this painting. Just off center to the right Balla shows Marinetti in characteristic declamatory poses, wearing a red and green Futurist outfit in accordance with Balla's 1914 manifesto, *Anti-neutral Clothing*. The large encircled eye on the left, the two oval forms within the leftward moving arrow, as well as the "abstract" shapes on the right refer to the beauteous Marchesa Casati whose celebrated literary and artistic salon in Rome seems to have inspired this picture. Balla's lost relief portrait of the Marchesa, which apparently had moving parts, contained similar individualizing features (illustrated in *Archivi del futurismo*, vol. 2, no. 216, ill. p. 115).

24. GIACOMO BALLA

Self Portrait (Autoritratto). c. 1920
Ink on paper, 9¼ x 8¼"
u.c. "BALLA/FU/TU/RISTA"

PROVENANCE:

Luce Balla, Rome
Winston Collection, 1960

REFERENCE:

Dorazio, *Balla,* ill. on jacket in green

G-178

Maria Blanchard 1881-1932

Born in Santander, Spain. 1906 went to Paris; Andre Lhôte introduced her to Cubist painters. 1913 returned to Spain. 1916 settled in Paris; established close contacts with Gris, Metzinger, Lipchitz and Rivera. Works emphasize contours of forms with freely modeled surfaces; style is geometric but never totally abstract. 1919 work became more realistic, though Cubist structure retained. Portrayed men and women in scenes from daily life and solitary children. Palette of earth colors heightens melancholic feeling. Died in Paris.

25. MARIA BLANCHARD

Composition with Figure (Composition avec Personnage). 1916
Oil on canvas, 51 x 37¾"
Unsigned

PROVENANCE:

Van Leer, Amsterdam
Galerie de l'Institut, Paris
Winston Collection, 1956

EXHIBITIONS:

Galerie de l'Institut, Paris, November 18-December 14, 1955, *Maria Blanchard Période Cubiste,* no. 10, p. 7, ill. p. 15
D.I.A., 1957-58, no. 15, p. 38, ill. p. 40

REFERENCE:

Degand and Arp, *Aujourd'hui,* 1957, p. 31

Umberto Boccioni 1882-1916

Born in Reggio Calabria. 1897 completed studies at Istituto Tecnico, Catania; moved to Rome c. 1900. 1901 with Severini worked in Balla's studio. Travelled extensively in Italy; 1906, 1908 visited Paris; 1906 to Russia. Late 1907 settled in Milan. With help of Carrà and Russolo wrote two Futurist painting manifestos, 1910. Became the leading figure and spokesman of Futurists' artists' wing: numerous influential theoretical writings. *Pittura, scultura futuriste (dinamismo plastico)*, published 1914. From 1911-12 created important sculpture. By late 1913 had begun to turn toward Cézanne. Enlisted and fought at front with other Futurists, killed during cavalry exercises in Verona.

Self Portrait (Autoritratto). c. 1908

Oil on canvas, 20¼ x 27″

l.r. "Boccioni"

PROVENANCE:

Raffaela Callegari-Boccioni, Verona
Winston Collection, 1958

EXHIBITION:

Museum of Modern Art, 1961, *Futurism*, no. 21, p. 142

REFERENCES:

Falqui, Enrico, *Bibliografia e iconografia del futurismo*, Sansoni, Florence, 1959, Tav. VI, p. 15
Kramer, Hilton, "Futurism Today," *Arts Magazine*, vol. 36, no. 1, October 1961, ill. p. 22
Archivi del futurismo, vol. 2, no. 55, p. 255, ill. p. 187
Ballo, *Boccioni*, 1964, no. 22, ill. p. 435
Calvesi, Maurizio, "Il manifesto del futurismo e i pittori futuristi," *L'Arte moderna*, vol. V, no. 37, 1967, ill. p. 38
Archivi del divisionismo, vol. 2, no. 2220, p. 182, pl. 465
Bruno, Gianfranco, *L'Opera completa di Boccioni*, Rizzoli, Milan, 1969, no. 16a, ill. p. 88 (hereafter cited as Bruno, *Boccioni*)

W-15

27. UMBERTO BOCCIONI

The Street Pavers (I Selciatori). 1911

Oil on canvas, 39⅜ x 39⅜"

l.l. "U B"

PROVENANCE:

Romeo Toninelli, Milan
Carlo Cardazzo, Galleria d'Arte del Naviglio, Milan
Winston Collection, 1954

EXHIBITIONS:

Galleria Centrale d'Arte (Palazzo Cova), Milan, December 28, 1916-January 14, 1917, *Grande Esposizione Boccioni, Pittore e Scultore Futurista*, no. 10
Bottega di Poesia, Milan, March 10-21, 1924, *Umberto Boccioni*, no. 13
The Museum of Modern Art, New York, June 28-September 18, 1949, *XX Century Italian Art*, pp. 9, 126, pl. 1, p. 35
XXVI Biennale, Venice, June 14-October 19, 1952, no. 50, p. 396
University of Michigan, 1955, no. 7, ill. p. 9
D.I.A., 1957-58, no. 16, p. 88
Museum of Modern Art, 1961, *Futurism*, no. 31, pp. 43, 142, ill. p. 44
D.I.A., 1972-73

REFERENCES:

Carrieri, Raffaele, *Pittura scultura d'avanguardia (1890-1950) in Italia*, Conchiglia, Milan, 1950, ill. p. 16
Valsecchi, Marco, *Umberto Boccioni*, Cavallino, Venice, 1950, ill., n.p.
Argan, Guilio Carlo, *Umberto Boccioni*, De Luca, Rome, 1953, pl. 20
"The Winston Collection on Tour," *Arts,* 1958, ill. p. 37
De Grada, Raffaele, *Boccioni, il mito del moderno,* Club del libro, Milan, 1962, tav. IX, pp. 158, 173, 178
"The Best in Art," *Arts Yearbook,* 6, 1962, p. 162
Archivi del futurismo, vol. 2, no. 197, p. 263, ill. p. 208
Winston, *Aujourd'hui,* 1962, ill. p. 5
Carrieri, Raffaele, *Futurism,* Milione, Milan, 1963, p. 187, pl. 1
Taylor, *Collections,* 1963, ill. p. 294
Ballo, *Boccioni,* 1964, no. 580, pl. XLV, pp. 373, 471
Martin, 1968, p. 105 f, 158 note 2, pl. 73
Archivi del divisionismo, 1968, vol. 2, no. 2447, p. 197, pl. 506
Bruno, *Boccioni,* no. 178, p. 114, pl. LV
Baro, *The Collector in America,* 1971, p. 181
Apollonio, Umbro, ed. *Futurist Manifestos,* Viking, New York 1972, no. 93, p. 229, ill. p. 168

W-22

A date of 1914 has frequently been given to this powerful work, but both the subject and its interpretation suggest an earlier execution, probably during the summer of 1911. The theme of a worker is thus directly related to Boccioni's hymn to labor, *The City Rises* of 1910-11 at The Museum of Modern Art, New York. He did not return to this subject in later years. Furthermore, the multiple image of one man seen from different points of view is an early attempt at presenting an image of continuing motion that was subsequently rejected in favor of a more synthetic form. Lastly, the still hesitant and superficial allusions to Cubism found here, suggest that only a second-hand knowledge of this approach was available to Boccioni at the time. Nonetheless, these vigorous street pavers with their sharp, angular movements and clanking sounds are worthy younger brothers of Courbet's *Stone Breakers* of 1849, which he may well have seen at the 1910 Venice Biennale.

*Anti-Graceful; The Mother; Portrait of the Artist's Mother
(Antigrazioso; Le Madre; Ritratto della madre).* 1912
Bronze, 24″ high

PROVENANCE:

Benedetta Marinetti, Rome
Winston Collection, 1956

EXHIBITIONS:

D.I.A., 1957-58, no. 20, p. 38, ill. p. 42
Milan, *Arte italiana,* no. 41, p. 194, ill. p. 51
Musée Nationale d'Art Moderne, Paris, October 20, 1960-
January 20, 1961, *Les Sources du XXème siècle,* no. 36, p. 24
Museum of Modern Art, 1961, *Futurism,* no. 48, pp. 87, 92,
143, ill. p. 91
D.I.A., 1972-73

REFERENCES:

Curjel, Hans, "Bemerkungen zum Futurismus," *Das Kunst-
werk,* vol. V, no. 3, 1951, ill. p. 13
Argan, Giulio Carlo, *Umberto Boccioni,* De Luca, Rome,
1953, pl. 42
Giedion-Welcker, Carola, *Contemporary Sculpture,*
Wittenborn, New York, 1960, ill. p. 85
Degand and Arp, *Aujourd'hui,* 1957, ill. p. 30
Saarinen, *Art News,* 1957, fig. 5, p. 65, ill. p. 34
"The Winston Collection on Tour," *Arts,* 1958, ill. p. 36
Francastel, Pierre, "Il futurismo e il suo tempo," *La
Biennale di Venezia,* vol. IX, nos. 36-37, July-December
1959, ill. p. 7
Seuphor, Michel, *La Sculpture de ce siècle,* Griffon, Neu-
châtel, Switzerland, 1959, p. 358, ill. p. 40. Published in
English as *The Sculpture of this Century,* Braziller, New
York, 1960 (hereafter cited as Seuphor, *Sculpture of this
Century,* 1960)
Pearlstein, Philip, "Futurism and Some Other Corrupt
Forms," *Art News,* vol. 60, no. 4, Summer 1961, ill. p. 30
De Grada, Raffaele, *Boccioni, Il mito del moderno,* Club
del libro, Milan, 1962, Tav. 74, 75; pp. 101, 140, 146, 175,
177, 343
Winston, *Aujourd'hui,* 1962, ill. p. 6
Barr, Margaret Scolari, *Medardo Rosso,* Museum of Modern
Art, New York, 1963, p. 63, ill. p. 62 (hereafter cited as Barr,
Rosso, 1963)
Taylor, *Collections,* 1963, p. 303
Ballo, *Boccioni,* 1964, no. 477, p. 500
Bowness, Alan, *Modern Sculpture,* Dutton, London, 1965,
ill. p. 125

Francoeur, *Chicago Mid-West Art,* 1967, ill. on cover
Licht, Fred, *Sculpture 19th and 20th Centuries: A History of
Western Sculpture,* New York Graphic Society, Greenwich,
1967, p. 332, pl. 220
Arnason, H. H., *History of Modern Art: Painting-Sculpture-
Architecture,* Abrams, New York, 1968, fig. 374, ill. p. 215
Martin, 1968, pp. 164, 167 f., pl. 151
Bruno, *Boccioni,* p. 108
Marrits, Louis E., *Modeled Portrait Sculpture,* A. S. Barnes,
South Brunswick, New Jersey, 1970, ill. p. 344
Golding, John, *Boccioni's Unique Forms of Continuity in
Space,* University of Newcastle-upon-Tyne, Newcastle-
upon-Tyne, 1972, p. 16, ill. p. 17
Rye, Jane, *Futurism,* Studio Vista, London, 1972, ill. p. 82

W-20

Boccioni's mother, like Cézanne's patient wife, was the
model and point of departure for many of his most searching
efforts. She was the sitter for at least one other sculpture, the
destroyed half-length *Testa + casa + luce (Head + House
+ Light)* of 1912, and for numerous paintings, drawings,
and prints, as shown by the many examples in this collection.
This is the only cast from the original plaster now in the
Galleria Nazionale d'Arte Moderna, Rome. It was made in
1950-51 by Fratelli Perego, Fonderia Artistica, Milan.

29. UMBERTO BOCCIONI

Development of a Bottle in Space (Still Life) (Sviluppo di una bottiglia nello spazio) (Natura morta)). 1912-13
Bronze, 15 x 24″
Unsigned

PROVENANCE:

Benedetta Marinetti, Rome
Winston Collection, 1957

EXHIBITIONS:

D.I.A., 1957-58, no. 21, p. 38, ill. p. 44
Los Angeles County Museum of Art, December 15, 1970-
February 21, 1971, *The Cubist Epoch,* no. 9, pp. 232, 275, pl.
294, p. 295. In collaboration with The Metropolitan Museum
of Art, New York, April 7-June 7, 1971 (hereafter cited as
The Cubist Epoch, 1970-71)
D.I.A., 1972-73

REFERENCES:

Argan, Giulo Carlo, *Umberto Boccioni,* De Luca, Rome,
1953, pl. 55
Saarinen, *Art News,* 1957, p. 65, ill. p. 64
Mellquist, *XXᵉ Siècle,* 1958, ill., n.p.
Canaday, John, *Mainstreams of Modern Art,* Holt, Rinehart
and Winston, New York, 1959, no. 632, pp. 473, 500, ill.
p. 501
Seuphor, *Sculpture of this Century,* 1960, p. 358, ill. p. 358
Taylor, *Collections,* 1963, p. 295
Bowness, Alan, *Modern Sculpture,* Dutton, New York, 1965,
ill. p. 126
Barilli, Renato, *La scultura del novecento,* Fabbri, 1968,
pl. 28, pp. 46-47
Kramer, Hilton, "The Cubist Epoch," *Art in America,* vol.
59, no. 2, March-April 1971, ill. p. 54

W-26

Boccioni made three sculptures of bottles, but only this one
has survived. His first dynamic still life is found in the important but lost painting of a city-scene, *Visioni simultanee
(Simultaneous Visions)* of 1911 *(Archivi del futurismo,* vol.
2, no. 278, ill. p. 223)
Of the original plaster, now in the Museu de Arte Contemporânea de São Paulo, four bronze casts were made: two
in 1931 by Gaetano Chiurazzi, Rome, now in the Civica
Galleria d'Arte Moderna, Milan, and The Museum of
Modern Art, New York, and two in 1949 by Giovanni and
Angelo Nicci, Rome, now in the Kunsthaus Zürich and
this collection. Another cast is in the collection of
Dr. Gianni Mattioli, Milan.

30. UMBERTO BOCCIONI

Unique Forms of Continuity in Space (Forme uniche della continuità nello spazio). 1913

Bronze, 48½ x 34″, including base

Unsigned

PROVENANCE:

Benedetta Marinetti, Rome
Winston Collection, 1956

EXHIBITIONS:

D.I.A., 1957-58, no. 18, p. 38, ill. on front and back cover
D.I.A., 1969, *Detroit Collects,* no. 27
D.I.A., 1972-73

REFERENCES:

Degand and Arp, *Aujourd'hui,* 1957, ill. p. 30
Vassar Alumnae Magazine, 1958, ill. p. 11
Seuphor, *Sculpture of This Century,* 1960, p. 358, ill. p. 43
Carrieri, Raffaele, "Boccioni peintre de sensations," *XXᵉ Siècle,* Nouvelle Série, XXIIIᵉ année, no. 17, Noël, 1961, p. 66
Kuh, Katherine, "Landmarks of Modern Art," *Saturday Review,* January 27, 1962, p. 00, ill.
Winston, *Aujourd'hui,* 1962, ill. p. 5
Taylor, *Collections,* 1963, pp. 302, 303, ill.
Bowness, Alan, *Modern Sculpture,* Dutton, London, 1965, ill. p. 72
Kuh, Katherine, *Break-Up: The Core of Modern Art,* New York Graphic Society, Greenwich, 1965, no. 30, p. 135, ill. p. 51
Baro, *Art in America,* 1967, ill. p. 72
Rye, Jane, *Futurism,* Studio Vista, London, 1972, ill. p. 89

W-24

The theme of the strenuously active, moving figure engaged Boccioni's best efforts during the peak years of his career. A series of monumental paintings, drawings, and four sculptures reveal his consuming desire to give new life to the ancient subject of the nude, which in 1910 was banned for ten years from the Futurist vocabulary. This is the fourth and final of the sculpted striding figures. The other three, indicative of the rigorous self-criticism to which he subjected his work, were destroyed after his death. *(Archivi del futurismo,* vol. 2, nos. 328-331, ill. p. 232)

Four bronze castings were made from the original plaster, now in the collection of the Museu de Arte Contemporânea de São Paulo: two in 1931 by Gaetano Chiurazzi, Rome, now in the Civica Galleria d'Arte Moderna, Milan, and The Museum of Modern Art, New York, and two in 1949 by Giovanni and Angelo Nicci, Rome, now in this collection and that of Paolo Marinotti, Milan. The earlier edition did not include the flat double base of the original plaster.

In 1972 the Galleria La Medusa, Rome, commissioned a further edition of eight bronze casts, but it is not known whether they were taken from the earlier editions or, more unlikely, from the original plaster. Another cast is in the collection of Dr. Gianni Mattioli, Milan.

31. UMBERTO BOCCIONI

Study for "The Drinker" (Studio per "Il Bevitore"). 1914

Oil, gouache, and collage on paper, 11½ x 14½"

l.r. "Boccioni"

PROVENANCE:

Neumann Galerie, Berlin
Ruggero Vasari, Berlin, 1922
Winston Collection, 1958

EXHIBITION:

Museum of Modern Art, 1961, *Futurism,* no. 64, p. 144

REFERENCES:

Archivi del futurismo, vol. 2, no. 379, p. 272, ill. p. 242
Taylor, *Collections,* 1963, p. 303
Ballo, *Boccioni,* 1964, no. 574, p. 481, pl. 183, p. 258
Baro, *Art in America,* 1967, ill. p. 72
Miesel, *The Connoisseur,* 1968, ill. p. 260
Bruno, *Boccioni,* no. 181b, ill. p. 115

W-18

Boccioni's early evolution, unlike that of most other major artists, lacked exposure to Cézanne and African sculpture. A meaningful encounter with both occurred only during the climactic years of Futurism. This collage is a singularly frank, if anxious, statement of Boccioni's creative process. The artist is trying to appropriate a Cézannian content as well as Picasso's "Africanized" interpretation of Cézanne's space and form, while seeking to imbue both with some Futurist meaning.

The painting to which this work is related is in the collection of Dr. Riccardo Jucker, Milan.

Constantin Brancusi 1876-1957

Born in Hobitza, Rumania. 1887 went to Tirgu Jiu. 1895
Craiova School of Arts and Crafts, Rumania, graduated
1898. 1902 diploma Bucharest School of Fine Arts. 1904
settled in Paris. 1905-07 attended Ecole des Beaux Arts,
Paris. Exhibited *Salon d'Automne* where he met Rodin in
1906. 1907 abandoned realism and began to develop mature,
abstract style. 1913 five works in Armory Show, New York.
1926, 1933 one-man shows Brummer Galleries, New York.
Travels included 1926 New York; 1938 Egypt, The Netherlands, Rumania; 1939 New York. 1955-56 retrospective,
Guggenheim Museum. 1956 became French citizen. Willed
studio to Musée National d'Art Moderne, Paris.

The Blond Negress (La Négresse blonde). 1933
Polished bronze and stone, head 15⅞″ h; 2 bases, each
12⅝″ h, total 41⅛″ h
Under lip "C Brancusi"; under head "Brancusi"

PROVENANCE:

the artist, Paris
Winston Collection, 1952

EXHIBITIONS:

University of Michigan, 1955, no. 9, p. 10
D.I.A., 1957-58, no. 22, p. 39, ill. p. 43
The Toledo Museum of Art, March 6-27, 1960, *What is
Modern Art?*
D.I.A., 1972-73

REFERENCES:

Degand and Arp, *Aujourd'hui,* 1957, ill. p. 30
Saarinen, *Art News,* 1957, p. 65
Vassar Alumnae Magazine, 1958, ill. p. 11
Giedion-Welcker, Carola, *Constantin Brancusi, 1876-1957,*
Braziller, New York, 1959, pl. 19, p. 69
Seuphor, *Sculpture of this Century,* 1960, p. 358, ill. p. 60
Taylor, *Collections,* 1963, pp. 298-99
Geist, Sidney, "Brancusi Catalogued," *Arts Magazine,* vol.
38, no. 4, January 1964, pp. 70-71
Geist, Sidney, "Letters to Editor," *Art Bulletin,* vol. XLVII,
no. 3-4, September-December 1966, pp. 462-63
Spear, Athena Tacha, "A Contribution to Brancusi Chron-
ology," *Art Bulletin,* vol. XLVIII, no. 1, March 1966, pp.
48-49
Geist, Sidney, *Constantin Brancusi, 1876-1957: A Retrospec-
tive Exhibition,* The Solomon R. Guggenheim Museum, New
York, 1969, p. 128, ill.

W-127

This bronze, according to Sidney Geist, is one of two after
The Art Institute of Chicago's marble *White Negress II* of
1928. Although the artist said 1926 was its date, Geist, based
on stylistic analysis and studies of Brancusi's casting
procedures, dates it 1933. Brancusi sometimes gave all
versions of one sculpture the same date, using the earliest
date to represent the conception of the idea.

Georges Braque 1882-1963

Born in Argenteuil, France. Began career as apprentice house painter. Studied Ecole des Beaux Arts, Le Havre and Paris until 1904. 1907 exhibited as Fauve in *Salon des Indépendants*. 1908 discarded Fauve palette in favor of Cubist color and geometry. 1909 established Cubist style with Picasso. Fought in World War I, received a head wound. By 1922 paintings returned to nature retaining only certain aspects of Cubism. 1933 first important retrospective in Basel. Worked in isolation throughout the War, 1948 published *Cahiers de Georges Braque: 1917-47*. 1948 first prize Venice Biennale. 1948-49 major exhibition The Museum of Modern Art and Cleveland Museum. From late 50's until his death, he continued to work in seclusion despite failing health.

33. GEORGES BRAQUE

Cards and Dice. 1914?
Oil on canvas, 14½ x 21", oval
Unsigned

PROVENANCE:

the artist
Marius de Zayas
Arthur B. Davies, Paris
Mrs. Morris Hillquit, New York, 1929
Jacques Seligmann & Co., New York, 1948
Winston Collection, 1948 (through Rose Fried)

EXHIBITIONS:

Pennsylvania Academy of Fine Arts, Philadelphia, April 17-May 9, 1920, *Exhibition of Paintings and Drawings of Representative Modern Masters*, no. 3, p. 5
Cranbrook, 1951, no. 2
University of Michigan, 1955, no. 10, p. 10
D.I.A., 1957-58, no. 23, p . 39, ill. p. 44
The Cubist Epoch, 1970-71, no. 33, p. 278, pl. 216, p. 194
D.I.A., 1972-73

REFERENCES:

Degand and Arp, *Aujourd'hui*, 1957, ill. p. 30
Vassar Alumnae Magazine, 1958, ill. p. 11

W-2

Cooper dates the painting 1914 (*The Cubist Epoch*, no. 33, p. 278), which is earlier than the frequently cited 1915-16; the latter is certainly less likely since Braque was severely wounded in 1915 and did not resume painting until 1917. Since the artist had introduced a pointillist technique into his general style by 1913-14, the earlier date is further substantiated.

Alexander Calder b. 1898

Born in Philadelphia. 1919 graduated as mechanical engineer from Stevens Institute of Technology in Hoboken, New Jersey. 1922 began studies at Art Students' League, New York. 1926 travelled to Paris; created circus figures, animated toys and wire sculpture. 1927 first one-man exhibition Weyhe Gallery, New York; began to divide his time between United States and France. 1930 after visit to Mondrian's studio in Paris, turned to abstraction. First abstract sculpture christened "stabiles" by Arp; later Marcel Duchamp called his moving sculptures "mobiles." Lives in Roxbury, Connecticut and Saché, France.

34. ALEXANDER CALDER

Mobile. 1949
Painted metal, 90 x 52 x 60″

PROVENANCE:

the artist
Winston Collection, 1949

EXHIBITIONS:

Cranbrook, 1951, no. 87
D.I.A., 1957-58, no. 24, p. 39. Did not travel

REFERENCES:

Saarinen, *Art News,* 1957, p. 33, ill. p. 32
Baro, *Art in America,* 1967, ill. p. 72

W-72

This work was made especially for the Winston's stairwell by Calder, although he never saw the location. As a consequence, a great deal of correspondence took place between the Winstons and the artist in a mutual effort to describe and understand the problems of space which were involved in the undertaking.

Carlo Carrà 1881-1966

Born in Quargnento, Piedmont. Trained as mural decorator;
1895 to Milan. Worked on decorations for International
Exposition, Paris, 1900. 1905-09 studied at Brera Academy.
Around 1908 friendship with Boccioni; formulated Futurist
painting manifestos of 1910 with him. More drawn to
Cubism than other Milanese Futurists were. Many contributions to literature of Futurism, most notably
Guerrapittura, 1915. 1916 or 17 met de Chirico; joined
with him in "metaphysical painting." Subsequent work
marked by mixture of primitivism and classicism and
rejection of dynamism of Futurist painting. 1920's association
with *Novecento* group of figurative painters. Died in Milan.

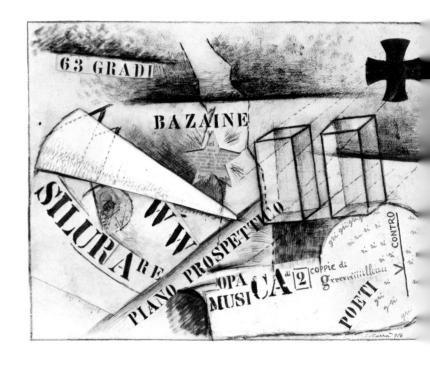

35. CARLO CARRA

The Night of January 20, 1915, I Dreamed This Picture
(Joffre's Angle of Penetration on the Marne Against Two
German Cubes) (La notte del 20 gennaio 1915 sognai questo
quadro (Angolo penetrante de Joffre sur Marne contro 2
cubi germanici)). 1915
Collage, gouache, ink and charcoal on paper, 10 x 13½"
l.r. "C. Carrà 914" (Inscription added later by artist)

PROVENANCE:

The New Gallery, New York
Winston Collection, 1960

EXHIBITIONS:

The Museum of Modern Art, New York, October 2-
November 12, 1961, *The Art of Assemblage,* no. 29, ill.
p. 155. Travelled to Dallas Museum of Contemporary Art,
January 9-February 11, 1962; San Francisco Museum of
Art, March 5-April 15, 1962 (hereafter cited as Museum of
Modern Art, 1961-62, *The Art of Assemblage)*
Guggenheim, 1963-64, *Twentieth Century Master*
Drawings, no. 19, pl. 12
D.I.A., 1972-73

REFERENCES:

Carrà, Carlo, *Guerrapittura,* Poesia, Milan, 1915, pl. 10, p. 29
"Un Demi-siècle d'art Italien," *Cahiers d'Art,* 1950, vol.
XXV, no. 1, ill. p. 84
Carrieri, Raffaele, *Futurism,* Milione, Milan, 1963, pl. 67
Taylor, *Collections,* 1963, p. 303
Johnson, Una E., *20th Century Drawings; Part I: 1900-1940,*
Shorewood, New York, 1964, pl. 31, p. 63
Martin, 1968, p. 200, pl. 213.

W-39

This handsome collage, like some of the other illustrations
in *Guerrapittura,* conveys Carrà's estrangement from
Futurism and predicts both Dada and the enigmatic and
calm imagery of his metaphysical painting of 1917 onward.
Purportedly evoking the most extreme Futurist moment of
actual war, Carrà has given the thrusts and shouts of
combat a dream-like distance and paradoxical meaning. His
forms are more precise and solid, and suggest that the
dynamic dispersion of the Futurist esthetic no longer seems
to apply.

Robert Delaunay 1885-1941

Born in Paris. 1902 apprenticed to set designer Ronsin. 1904 first paintings, influenced by Impressionists and Pont-Aven group: exhibited at *Salon d'Automne* and *Salon des Indépendents*. Studied color theories of Chevreul. Friendship with Rousseau, Metzinger. 1910 married painter Sonia Terck; showed at first *Blaue Reiter* exhibition, Munich. 1910-11 met Apollinaire and Gleizes; Cubist period. 1912 Apollinaire coined term *Orphisme* to describe Delaunay's personal idiom emphasizing color, light and motion. 1912 "constructive" period, characterized by works organized through colored planes and their "simultaneous contrasts"; series of paintings of chromatically dissected circular forms, among best known works. Continued emphasis on color, light and motion in figurative works of 20's and abstract paintings of 30's.

36. ROBERT DELAUNAY

Still Life with Red Tablecloth (Nature morte à la nappe rouge). 1937
Oil on canvas, 46⅜ x 39⅜"
Unsigned

PROVENANCE:

Sonia Delaunay, Paris
Winston Collection, 1953

EXHIBITIONS:

Galerie Louis Carré, Paris, December 17, 1946-January 17, 1947, *Robert Delaunay, 1885-1941,* no. 20
Galerie J. H. Bernheim-Jeune, Paris, December 16, 1950-January 12, 1951, *Rythmes et couleurs,* no. 5
University of Michigan, 1955, no. 12, p. 10
D.I.A., 1957-58, no. 29. p. 45, ill. p. 47
D.I.A., 1972-73

REFERENCES:

Taylor, *Collections,* 1963, p. 303
Baro, *Art in America,* 1967, p. 72

W-150

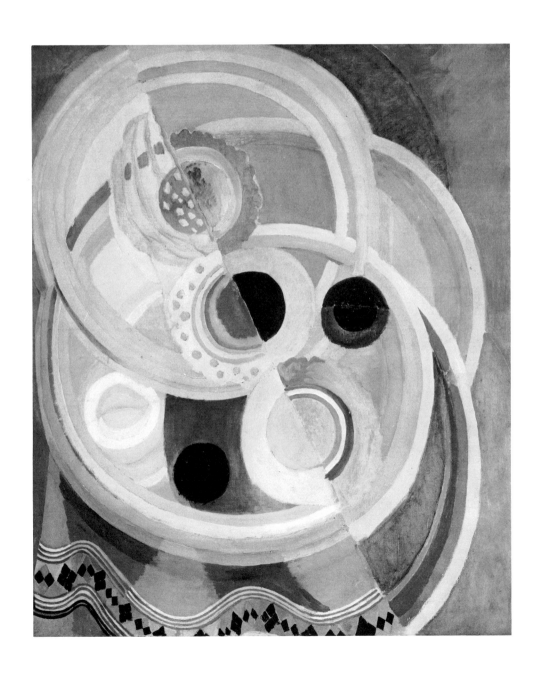

Theo van Doesburg 1883-1931

Born C.E.M. Küpper in Utrecht. 1899 began painting. 1908
first shown at The Hague. 1917 founded *De Stijl* periodical
whose contributors, Mondrian, Oud, Wils, Bart van der
Leck, Vantongerloo, formed the *De Stijl* movement which
stressed the need for abstraction and simplification, producing compositions based on geometric figures and primary
colors. After 1917 propagandized for *De Stijl* in Belgium,
France, Italy, Spain, Czechoslovakia and Germany. Lec-
tured at Bauhaus. Friendship with Schwitters led to interest
in Dada; wrote poems under pseudonym I.K. Bonset. 1926
published *Manifesto of Elementarism* broadening the principles of *De Stijl*.

Still Life. 1916
Oil on canvas, 13 ⅞ x 15 ⅞"
Unsigned

PROVENANCE:

Nelly van Doesburg, Meudon
The Pinacotheca Gallery, New York
Winston Collection, 1949

EXHIBITIONS:

Art of this Century, New York, April 29-May 31, 1947,
Theo van Doesburg, no. 16. Travelled to San Francisco
Museum of Art, July 29-August 24, 1947
The Pinacotheca Gallery, New York, March 22-April 21,
1949, no. 2
Cranbrook, 1951, no. 55
University of Michigan, 1955, no. 14, p. 10
D.I.A., 1957-58, no. 31, p. 45, ill. p. 17
The Albright-Knox Art Gallery, Buffalo, March 3-April
14, 1968 *Plus By Minus: Today's Half-Century,* no. 30, ill.
D.I.A., 1972-73

REFERENCES:

"The Winston Collection on Tour," *Arts,* 1958, ill. p. 35
Seuphor, Michel, *Abstract Painting: Fifty Years of Accom-
plishment, from Kandinsky to the Present,* Abrams, New
York, 1962, no. 67, p. 303 (hereafter cited as Seuphor,
Abstract Painting, 1962)
Baro, *Art in America,* 1967, ill. p. 74

W-74

Max Ernst b. 1891

Born in Bruehl, near Cologne. Studied University of Bonn. 1919 launched Cologne Dada movement with Arp and Baargeld. 1922 moved to Paris; collaborated in founding of Surrealist movement. 1935 began working in sculpture. 1941 came to New York; married Peggy Guggenheim. After 1945 lived in Sedona, Arizona with his second wife, painter Dorothea Tanning. 1952 returned to Paris. 1958 became French citizen. 1959 major retrospective at Musée National d'Art Moderne, Paris. Lives and works in Paris and south of France.

38. MAX ERNST

Sitting Buddha (Sitzender Buddha). 1920
Collage on paper, 7⅞ x 8⅛″
bottom "sitzender buddha (démandez votre médecin) max ernst / 20"

PROVENANCE:

Tristan Tzara, Paris
Winston Collection, 1954

EXHIBITIONS:

Sidney Janis Gallery, New York, April 15-May 9, 1953, *Dada,* no. 91
D.I.A., 1957-58, p. 59. Did not travel

G-179

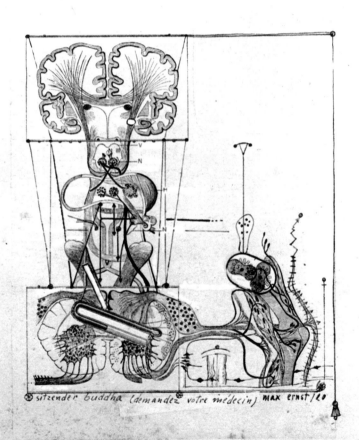

sitzender buddha (demandez votre médecin) MAX ERNST/20

39. MAX ERNST

Composition. 1924-26
Oil on canvas, 10½ x 9″
l.r. "Max Ernst"

PROVENANCE:

Rose Fried Gallery, New York
Winston Collection, 1955

EXHIBITIONS:

Rose Fried Gallery, New York, October 17-November 26,
1955, *30 Works by 17 Masters,* no. 9
D.I.A., 1957-58, no. 38, p. 38, ill. p. 32

REFERENCES:

"The Winston Collection on Tour," *Arts,* 1958, ill. p. 38
Seuphor, *Abstract Painting,* 1962, no. 124, p. 303, ill. p. 91
Baro, *Art in America,* 1967, ill. p. 72

W-138

40. MAX ERNST

Come into the Continents. 1926
Pencil and crayon on paper, 16½ x 10″
l.r. "Max Ernst"

PROVENANCE:

Galerie Rive Gauche, Paris
Winston Collection, 1952

EXHIBITIONS:

University of Michigan, 1955, no. 17, p. 11
D.I.A., 1957-58, no. 37, p. 48. Did not travel
Indiana University, 1971, *Reflection*, no. 52, pp. 12, 49, ill.
p. 12

G-177

This drawing is related to plates XIX and XXII of portfolio,
Histoire Naturelle, Paris, 1926 (Ellen Sharp, *Reflection,*
1971, p. 12)

Paul Feeley 1910-1966

Born in Des Moines, Iowa. 1922 began studying painting, Palo Alto, California. 1931 moved to New York; studied at Art Students' League; joined Mural Painters Society of New York. Supported himself by decorating restaurants, hotels and nightclubs. 1935 teacher at Cooper Union Art School. 1939-43 teacher at Bennington College in Vermont. 1943-46 served in Marine Corps. 1946 returned to Bennington where he taught until his death. 1951 contact with American avant-garde art. Style developed toward abstraction with an emphasis on color. Simple shapes create highly equivocal relationships between figure and ground. 1955 first major exhibit in New York at Tibor de Nagy Gallery. Died in New York. 1968 Memorial Exhibition, Guggenheim Museum, New York.

41. PAUL FEELEY

Katadoro. 1963
Oil and enamel on canvas, 66 x 51"
On reverse "Title: Katadoro/7 Feb. '63"

PROVENANCE:

the artist
Betty Parsons Gallery, New York
Winston Collection, 1964

EXHIBITIONS:

Betty Parsons Gallery, New York, May 13-31, 1963,
Paul Feeley
Betty Parsons Gallery, New York, October 27-November 21,
1964, *Paul Feeley*
The Solomon R. Guggenheim Museum, New York, April 11-
May 26, 1968, *Paul Feeley (1910-1966): A Memorial
Exhibition*, ill. p. 42
D.I.A., 1969, *Detroit Collects*, no. 59

W-225

Otto Freundlich 1878-1943

Born in Stolp, Pomerania, Germany. 1903 studied art history, Berlin and Munich. 1907-08 studied art, Berlin. 1908-09 Paris, studio at "Bateau Lavoir." 1910-13 exhibited in Paris, Berlin, Düsseldorf, Amsterdam. Hospital attendant in Cologne during World War I. 1914-18 worked on journal *Action;* member *November Group* under leadership of Pechstein, which believed in unity of arts, architecture and city planning under socialist state. 1924 returned to Paris. 1932 member *Abstraction-Création.* Participated in numerous European exhibitions. Art declared degenerate by Nazis. Persecution by Nazis; died in concentration camp.

42. OTTO FREUNDLICH

The Unity of Life and Death (L'Unité de la vie et de la mort). 1936-38
Oil on canvas, 47⅛ x 35½"
l.r. "F"; on reverse u.l. "28.IX / 1938"; l.c. "Otto Freundlich / Paris / 1936-38"; r.c. "Hommage / à Madame / Camille Lefèvre"; l.l. "L'Unité / de la Vie / et / de la Mort / commencé / mars 1936 / terminé Sept 38"

PROVENANCE:

Peggy Guggenheim, Venice
Nelly van Doesburg, Meudon
Winston Collection, 1954

EXHIBITIONS:

La Galerie Rive Droite, Paris, June 22-July 24, 1954, *Otto Freundlich, 1878-1943*
University of Michigan, 1955, no. 20, p. 11
D.I.A., 1957-58, no. 41, p. 48, ill. p. 49
D.I.A., 1972-73

REFERENCES:

Read, *Modern Painting,* 1959, no. 105, p. 354, ill. p. 305
Seuphor, *Abstract Painting,* 1962, no. 134, p. 304, ill. p. 98
Baro, *Art in America,* 1967, ill. p. 76
Arnason, H. H., *History of Modern Art: Painting, Sculpture, Architecture,* Abrams, New York, 1968, p. 403
Baro, *The Collector in America,* 1971, p. 182

W-158

Alberto Giacometti 1901-1966

Born in Stampa, Switzerland, son of the Neo-Impressionist
painter Augusto Giacometti. 1919 began studying sculpture
at Ecole des Arts et Métiers in Geneva. 1922 settled in Paris.
1922-25 studied with Bourdelle. Early abstract sculpture
reveals Cubist and primitive influence. 1929 joined Surrealist
group. Returned to the figure in mid 30's. 1932 first one-man
exhibition at Galerie Pierre Colle, Paris. 1955 retrospective
at Guggenheim Museum. 1965 retrospective at The Museum
of Modern Art, New York. Died in Coiro, Switzerland.

43. ALBERTO GIACOMETTI

The Couple; Man and Woman. 1926
Bronze, 23⅝ x 14½ x 7"
back of base u.r. "A. Giacometti 4/6"; l.l. "Susse Fondeur
Paris"
Fourth of six casts

PROVENANCE:

the artist
Galerie Maeght, Paris
Maurice Lafaille, Paris
Pierre Matisse Gallery, New York, November 1955
Winston Collection, December 1955

EXHIBITIONS:

D.I.A., 1957-58, no. 43, p. 52, ill. p. 51
The Museum of Modern Art, New York, June 7-October
10, 1965, *Alberto Giacometti,* no. 2, pp. 10, 115 (ill. of cast
from Museum of Fine Arts, Zurich, p. 33). Travelled to The
Art Institute of Chicago, November 5-December 12, 1965;
Los Angeles County Museum of Art, January 6-February
14, 1966; San Francisco Museum of Art, March 10-April
24, 1966

REFERENCES:

Lord, James, "Alberto Giacometti, sculpteur et peintre,"
L'Oeil, no. 1, January 15, 1955, ill. p. 18 (no indication of
which cast). Published in English in *The Selective Eye,*
Random House, New York, 1955, ill. p. 94
Lippard, Lucy R., "Max Ernst and a Sculpture of Fantasy,"
Art International, vol. XI, no. 2, February 20, 1967, ill. p. 38
Arnason, H. H., *History of Modern Art: Painting, Sculpture,
Architecture,* Abrams, New York, 1968, no. 627, p. 392, ill.
p. 393

W-84

Albert Gleizes 1881-1953

Born in Paris. Served as apprentice in his father's textile design studio. 1902 exhibited pointillist paintings at *Société Nationale des Beaux Arts*. 1906-08 became involved with Utopian Socialism and founded a free university and community of artists and writers, L'Abbaye de Créteil. 1911 arrived at own Cubist idiom. 1912 collaborated with Metzinger on treatise *Du Cubisme*. 1915, 1917-18 visited New York. Paintings of 1920's reveal his search for metaphysical principles of reality. Mid 1930's began lyrical abstraction of late style. Died in Avignon.

44. ALBERT GLEIZES

The Bather (La Baigneuse). 1912
Oil on canvas, 24 x 15″
l.l. "Alb Gleizes 12"

PROVENANCE:

Theodore Schempp, Paris
Earl L. Stendahl, Hollywood, California
Winston Collection, 1950

EXHIBITIONS:

Société Normande de Peinture Moderne, Rouen, opened May 6, 1912, no. 92
Stedelijk Museum, Amsterdam, October 6-November 7, 1912, *Moderne Kunst Kring*, no. 113
Cranbrook, 1951, no. 8
University of Michigan, 1955, no. 22, p. 11
D.I.A., 1957-58, no. 45, p. 52, ill. p. 51
The Solomon R. Guggenheim Museum, New York, September 14-November 1, 1964, *Albert Gleizes, 1881-1953: A Retrospective Exhibition,* in collaboration with Musée National d'Art Moderne, Paris and Museum am Ostwall, Dortmund, no. 30, p. 29, ill. p. 44. Did not travel
D.I.A., 1972-73

REFERENCES:

Degand and Arp, 1957, ill. p. 30
Vassar Alumnae Magazine, 1958, ill. p. 11
Taylor, *Collections,* 1963, ill. p. 303

W-174

Julio Gonzalez 1876-1942

Born in Barcelona, son of a goldsmith. 1892 studied painting, School of Fine Arts, Barcelona. 1900 exhibited metal work at the International Exhibition of Chicago; moved to Paris, met Picasso and produced pastels and paintings. 1908 deeply affected by the death of his brother Joan. 1917 slowly resumed work. 1926 first forged iron sculptures. 1929-31 assisted Picasso in welding iron sculptures. 1932 joined Constructivist group *Cercle et Carré*. 1937 *Montserrat* exhibited at Spanish Pavillion of World's Fair, Paris. 1940 gave up welding because of war; concentrated on drawing and molding in plaster.

45. JULIO GONZALEZ

Woman with Broom (La Femme au balai). 1929-30
Iron, 13 x 7¼ x 3½"
back left of base "J. Gonzalez"
Unique piece

PROVENANCE:

the artist, Paris
Mario Tozzi, Paris, c. 1930-34
Winston Collection, 1958

EXHIBITIONS:

Musée National d'Art Moderne, Paris, February 1-March 9, 1952, *Julio Gonzalez: Sculptures*, no. 36, p. 12
Stedelijk Museum, Amsterdam, April 7-May 10, 1955, *Julio Gonzalez,* no. 37, ill. Travelled to Palais des Beaux Arts, Brussels, May 20-June 19, 1955; Kunsthalle, Bern, July 2-August 7, 1955; Musée des Beaux Arts, La Chaux de Fonds, Switzerland (in Bern catalogue ill. fig. 37; not in catalogue listing)

REFERENCES:

Degand, Léon, *Gonzalez,* Universe Books, New York, 1959, no. 3, text reference, ill., n.p.
Seuphor, *Sculpture of this Century,* 1960, p. 80

W-118

46. JULIO GONZALEZ

The Kiss (Le Baiser). 1930
Iron, 10½ x 11¼ x 3″
back u.l. "J. Gonzalez / 1930"
Unique piece

PROVENANCE:

the artist, Paris
Mario Tozzi, Paris, c. 1930-34
Winston Collection, 1958

EXHIBITIONS:

Galerie de France, Paris, 1930, *Julio Gonzalez Sculptures*
Musée National d'Art Moderne, Paris, February 1-March 9, 1952, *Julio Gonzalez: Sculptures,* no. 42, p. 15
Stedelijk Museum, Amsterdam, April 7-May 10, 1955, *Julio Gonzalez,* no. 51, text reference, ill., n.p. Travelled to Palais des Beaux Arts, Brussels, May 20-June 19, 1955; Kunsthalle, Bern, July 2-August 7, 1955; Musée des Beaux Arts, La Chaux de Fonds, Switzerland (in Bern catalogue no. 27, ill. fig. 51)

REFERENCES:

Gindertael, R. V., "Gonzalez," *Cimaise,* série 3, no. 7-8, June-July-August 1956, pp. 5, 11, ill. p. 13
Degand, Léon, *Gonzalez,* Universe Books, New York, 1959, no. 4, text reference, ill., n.p.
Seuphor, *Sculpture of this Century,* 1960, p. 361, ill. p. 274

W-117

This is among the earliest of Gonzalez' abstract sculptures, and was executed during the time of his involvement with Picasso.

Man with a Guitar (L'Homme à la guitare). 1918

Pencil on paper, 14⅟₁₆ x 8⁵⁄₁₆″

Unsigned

PROVENANCE:

Jeanne Bucher, Paris
Julius Loeb, New York
Parke-Bernet Galleries, New York, 1947
Kleeman Galleries, New York, 1947
Buchholz Gallery, New York
Winston Collection, 1950

EXHIBITIONS:

Buchholz Gallery, New York, January 16-February 11, 1950, *Juan Gris,* no. 42
Buchholz Gallery, New York, September 26-October 4, 1950, *Contemporary Drawings,* no. 26, ill.
Cranbrook, 1951, no. 62
University of Michigan, 1955, no. 23, p. 11
D.I.A., 1957-58, no. 46. p. 52
The Museum of Modern Art, New York, April 9-June 1, 1958, *Juan Gris,* ill. p. 99. In collaboration with Minneapolis Institute of Arts, June 24-July 24, 1958; The San Francisco Museum of Art, August 11-September 14, 1958; Los Angeles County Museum of Art, September 29-October 26, 1958
D.I.A., 1962, *French Drawings and Watercolors*
Marlborough-Gerson Gallery, New York, November-December 1963, *Artist and Maecenas: A Tribute to Curt Valentin,* no. 147, ill. p. 80
Indiana University, 1971, *Reflection,* no. 60, p. 51, ill. p. 53
D.I.A., 1972-73

REFERENCE:

Julius Loeb Collection, Parke-Bernet Galleries, Inc., New York, Sale No. 835, February 6, 1947, no. 23, ill.

G-175

Juan Gris 1887-1927

Born in Madrid. 1902 School of Arts and Industry, Madrid. 1904 left school to study with José Maria Moreno Carbonero; did Art Nouveau book illustration. 1906 moved to "Bateau Lavoir" in Paris near Picasso. Met Apollinaire, Max Jacob, André Salmon. By 1911 painting in Analytic Cubist style. 1912 exhibited with Cubists at the *Section d'Or.* 1922-23 sets for Diaghilev ballets. 1923 first one-man exhibition Galerie Simon, Paris. 1924 delivered lecture on Cubism at the Sorbonne, *On the Possibilities of Painting.*

48. JUAN GRIS

The Siphon Bottle (Le Siphon). July 1919
Oil on canvas, 21$\frac{11}{16}$ x 18″
l.l. "Juan Gris/7-19"

PROVENANCE:

Pierre Faure, Paris
Léonce Rosenberg, Paris
Galerie Louise Leiris, Paris
Winston Collection, 1951

EXHIBITIONS:

Galerie Simon, Paris, March 20-April 15, 1923, *Juan Gris*
Kunsthaus, Zurich, April 2-26, 1933, *Juan Gris,* no. 92
Buchholz Gallery, New York, January 16-February 11, 1950,
Juan Gris, no. 17, ill.
Cranbrook, 1951, no. 9, ill.
University of Michigan, 1955, no. 24, p. 11, ill.
D.I.A., 1957-58, no. 47, p. 52, ill. p. 53
D.I.A., 1972-73

REFERENCES:

Degand and Arp, *Aujourd'hui,* 1957, ill. p. 30
Vassar Alumnae Magazine, 1958, ill. p. 11
Baro, *The Collector in America,* 1971, ill. p. 186

W-65

Auguste Herbin 1882-1960

Born in Quiévy, France. 1898-1901 Ecole des Beaux Arts, Lille. 1901 moved to Paris. 1905 exhibited Impressionist paintings at *Salon des Indépendents.* 1909 moved to "Bateau Lavoir" near Picasso, Braque and Gris. By 1913 was painting in Cubist style. By 1918 had rejected the object and was painting abstractions based on his personal pictorial language of color and form. 1931 co-founder with Vantongerloo of *Abstraction-Création* group. 1940's invented his "plastic alphabet." 1949 published his theories of color and form *L'art non-figuratif non-objectif;* founded *Salon des Réalités Nouvelles* where he exhibited until his death.

49. AUGUSTE HERBIN

Composition. January 1921
Oil on canvas, 18$\frac{13}{16}$ x 13$\frac{11}{16}$"
l.l. "herbin"; l.c. "janvier 1921"

PROVENANCE:

Léonce Rosenberg, Paris
Galerie Rive Gauche, Paris
Winston Collection, 1952

EXHIBITIONS:

University of Michigan, 1955, no. 26, p. 12, ill.
D.I.A., 1957-58, no. 51, p. 56, ill. p. 54
D.I.A., 1972-73

REFERENCE:

Baro, *The Collector in America,* 1971, ill. p. 182

W-161

Vasily Kandinsky 1866-1944

Born in Moscow. 1892 law degree University of Moscow.
1896 went to Munich to become a painter. 1901 founded
Phalanx group. 1909 settled in Murnau, organized *Neue
Künstlervereiningung.* 1910 wrote *On the Spiritual in Art*
in which he conceived of color and form as sole content of
painting. 1911 founded *Blaue Reiter* group with Franz Marc.
1917 returned to Russia; married his second wife Nina;
teacher and administrator of the arts until government hos-
tility forced him to leave. 1922 accepted post at Weimar
Bauhaus; 1926 Dessau Bauhaus; 1933 settled in Paris after
Nazis closed Bauhaus. Developed non-objective style in
Munich. During Bauhaus period utilized geometric forms.
In Paris years incorporated biomorphic forms of Miró and
Arp in his work.

50. VASILY KANDINSKY

Luminosity (Aufleuchten). 1927
Oil on canvas, 20½ x 13½"
l.l. with monogram "VK/27"

PROVENANCE:

Nierendorf Gallery, New York
Winston Collection, 1944

EXHIBITIONS:

Museum of Non-Objective Painting, New York, March 15-
May 15, 1945, *Kandinsky Memorial Exhibition,* no. 119
Cranbrook, 1951, no. 15, ill.
University of Michigan, 1955, no. 27, p. 12, ill.
D.I.A., 1957-58, no. 52, p. 56, ill. p. 54
D.I.A., 1972-73

REFERENCE:

Goldwater, Robert, *Space and Dream,* M. Knoedler & Co.,
New York, 1967, ill. p. 53 (hereafter cited as Goldwater,
Space and Dream, 1967)

W-75

51. VASILY KANDINSKY

De Profundis. 1932
Watercolor on paper, 18¼ x 12¹⁵⁄₁₆"
l.l. with monogram "VK/32"

PROVENANCE:

The Pinacotheca Gallery, New York
Winston Collection, 1948

EXHIBITIONS:

Cranbrook, 1951, no. 13
D.I.A., 1957-58, no. 54, p. 56. Did not travel
D.I.A., 1972-73

REFERENCE:

Kandinsky, Vasily, *Aus der Tiefe,* Paris, 1932, sketch no. 473.
Unpublished notebook

W-59

Paul Klee 1879-1940

Born in Münchenbuchsee, near Bern, of a musical family.
1898 art school in Munich. 1906 married and settled in
Munich. 1912 exhibited in second *Blaue Reiter* exhibition;
visited Delaunay's studio in Paris. 1914 travelled to Tunis
and Kairouan, influenced by Mediterranean light and color.
1920 began teaching at Weimar Bauhaus. 1924 founded
Blue Four with Kandinsky, Feininger and Jawlensky. 1925
publication of *Pedagogical Sketchbook*. 1926 moved to
Dessau. 1928 travelled to Egypt. 1929 one-man exhibition
Flechtheim Gallery, Berlin, which travelled to The Museum
of Modern Art, New York, 1930. 1931 left Bauhaus to
teach at Academy in Düsseldorf for two years. 1935 became
ill. Died in Muralto-Locarno, Switzerland.

52. PAUL KLEE

Forged Still Life. c. 1926
Watercolor on paper, 15⅛ x 17″
u.r. "Klee"

PROVENANCE:

Karl Nierendorf, New York
Winston Collection, 1944

EXHIBITIONS:

Cranbrook, 1951, no. 16, ill.
University of Michigan, 1955, no. 29
D.I.A., 1957-58, no. 55, p. 56
D.I.A., 1972-73

W-135

53. PAUL KLEE

What Remains (Was Blieb). 1937
Gouache with charcoal on paper, 9¾ x 13¼″
u.r. "Klee"; l.c. "1937 p. 18 was blieb"

PROVENANCE:

the artist
Jurg Spiller, Basel
Little Gallery, Birmingham, Michigan, c. 1955
Winston Collection, 1960

EXHIBITION:

Indiana University, 1971, *Reflection,* no. 82, p. 59, ill. p. 64

G-131

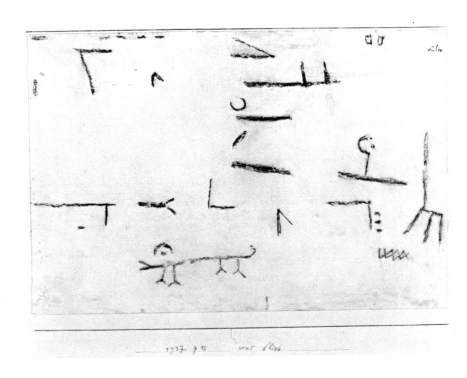

54. PAUL KLEE

Signs in Blue. c. 1938
Watercolor on tinted cloth, 12¹⁵⁄₁₆ x 10⅞″
u.l. "Klee"

PROVENANCE:

Nierendorf Gallery, New York
Winston Collection, 1947

EXHIBITIONS:

Cranbrook, 1951, no. 17
University of Michigan, 1955, no. 30, p. 12, ill.
D.I.A., 1957-58, no. 56, p. 56, ill. p. 55
D.I.A., 1972-73

W-3

Gaston Lachaise 1882-1935

Born in Paris. 1895 entered Ecole Bernard Palissy, Paris. 1895-1904 Académie Nationale des Beaux Arts. 1906 to Boston, worked for sculptor Henry Hudson Kitson assisting him on military monuments. 1912 to New York, worked independently on small human figures which became basis for subsequent monumental sculpture. 1913 became Paul Manship's assistant. 1918 first one-man exhibition Stephen Bourgeois Gallery, New York. Met Robert Henri, John Sloan, others. Influence of Nadelman, Hindu sculpture on his work. 1927 one-man exhibition at Steiglitz' Intimate Gallery, New York. Numerous commissions during career, executed portrait busts, massive nudes and series of sections of female nudes.

55. GASTON LACHAISE

(a) *Woman Arranging Hair.* c. 1910-12
Bronze, 10½ x 5 x 3¾″
base l.r. "Lachaise"; bottom "18"
(b) *Woman - Arms Akimbo.* c. 1910-12
Bronze, 11 x 5 x 5″
base l.r. "G.Lachaise"; bottom "12"

PROVENANCE:

Weyhe Gallery, New York
Winston Collection, 1956

EXHIBITIONS:

Weyhe Gallery, New York, December 22, 1955-January 28, 1956, *Drawings and Sculpture, Lachaise*
D.I.A., 1957-58, no. 57, p. 57. Did not travel
Los Angeles County Museum of Art, December 3, 1963-January 19, 1964, *Gaston Lachaise 1882-1935, Sculpture and Drawings,* no. 6 and 7, ill. Travelled to Whitney Museum of American Art, New York, February 18-April 5, 1964
J. B. Speed Art Museum, Louisville, October 16-November 28, 1965, *The Figure in Sculpture,* no. 8
Fine Arts Gallery, University of Wisconsin, Milwaukee, September 29-October 22, 1970, *Gaston Lachaise Sculpture Exhibition*

REFERENCES:

B.G. "A Season for Sculpture," *Arts,* vol. 30, no. 4, January 1956, ill. p. 22 (*Woman Arranging Hair* only)
T[yler], P[arker], "Reviews and Previews," *Art News,* vol. 54 no. 9, January 1956, ill. p. 50 (*Woman Arranging Hair* only)
Danieli, Fidel A., "Art Forms," *Daily Brush,* University of California, Los Angeles, December 11, 1963
The UWM Post, University of Wisconsin, Milwaukee, September 25, 1970, ill. p. 6

W-123, 122

Roger de La Fresnaye 1885-1925

Born in Le Mans, France. 1903 entered Académie Julian, Paris; 1904 and 1906-08 Ecole des Beaux Arts, Paris; 1908 studied with Denis and Sérusier. 1910 exhibited at *Salon des Indépendants* and *Salon d'Automne*. 1911 growing interest in Cubism; association with Puteaux Group which formed *Section d'Or*. Participated in *Section d'Or* exhibitions, 1911, 1912. 1914 first one-man exhibition Galerie Levesque, Paris. 1914 enlisted; 1918 discharged for ill health which continued until his death. 1920 abandoned Cubism for return to classical, realistic style.

Study for "The 14th of July" (Etude pour "Le Quatorze juillet"). 1913
Watercolor on paper, 16¾ x 23″
l.r. "R de la Fresnaye/1913"

PROVENANCE:

Galerie de Berri, Paris
Galerie Percier, Paris
Winston Collection, 1951

EXHIBITIONS:

Galerie de Berri, Paris, 1946 and 1949, no. 42
Musée National d'Art Moderne, Paris, 1950, no. 101, p. 33
Cranbrook, 1951, no. 23
Albion College, 1956, no. 16
D.I.A., 1957-58, no. 58, p. 57
Albright-Knox Art Gallery, Buffalo, September 26-October 22, 1967, *The Painters of The Section d'Or*, no. 18, pp. 28, 31, ill. p. 31
Indiana University, 1971, *Reflection*, no. 83, p. 60, ill. p. 65
D.I.A., 1972-73

REFERENCE:

Seligmann, Germain, *Roger de La Fresnaye: with a catalogue raisonné*, New York Graphic Society, Greenwich, 1969, no. 142, p. 158, ill. (hereafter cited as Seligmann, *de La Fresnaye*, 1969)

W-57

57. ROGER DE LA FRESNAYE

Composition with a Trumpet (Le Clairon et le tambour).
January 1918
Ink and wash on paper, 12¼ x 9⅜"
l.r. "R de la Fresnaye/Janv 18"

PROVENANCE:

Van der Klip, Paris
Galerie Percier, Paris
Winston Collection, 1951

EXHIBITIONS:

Cranbrook, 1951, no. 24
University of Michigan, 1955, no. 31, p. 12
D.I.A., 1957-58, no. 59, p. 57, ill. p. 55
D.I.A., 1962, *French Drawings and Watercolors*
D.I.A., 1972-73, ill. cover checklist

REFERENCE:

Seligmann, *de La Fresnaye,* 1969, no. 265, ill. p. 189

G-163

Henri Laurens 1881-1954

Born in Paris. Self-taught. Early influence of Rodin. 1904-10 studio in "Bateau Lavoir." 1911 formed life-long friendship with Braque. 1913 exhibited at *Salon des Indépendants.* 1915 began Cubist still-life constructions influenced by Picasso. 1915-18 *papiers collés.* 1918 began direct carving in stone and plaster modeling. Utilized technique of faceting and hollowing out, derived from Analytic Cubist painting style. After 1920 more conventional treatment of wood and stone. Around 1925 style, though still grounded in Cubism, became more organic. Exhibited at World's Fair, Paris, 1937. Female nudes his constant theme. Attenuated forms typical of work of 30's; massive, organic volumes mark sculpture of 40's. São Paulo Bienal 1953, awarded sculpture prize.

Man with a Moustache. 1919?

Stone, 17 x 5⅝ x 6″

l.r. front neck "H.L."

PROVENANCE:

Léonce Rosenberg, Paris
Yves le Delion, Paris, 1951
Jacques Ullman, Paris, 1951
Galerie Rive Gauche, Paris
Winston Collection, 1954

EXHIBITIONS:

University of Michigan, 1955, no. 32, p. 12, ill.
D.I.A., 1957-58, no. 60, p. 57, ill p. 58
The Cubist Epoch, 1971, no. 159, pp. 258, 293, pl. 324, p. 260
D.I.A., 1972-73

REFERENCES:

de Solier, René, "Uno Scultore tra due mondi: Henri Laurens," *La Biennale di Venezia,* October 1950, p. 14
Saarinen, *Art News,* 1957, p. 64
Taylor, *Collections,* 1963, p. 292
Baro, *Art in America,* 1967, p. 75

W-137

Although this piece has traditionally been dated 1917, Cooper dates it 1919 (*Cubist Epoch,* p. 258), as Laurens' earliest direct carving was done in 1918.

Fernand Léger 1881-1955

Born in Argentan, France. 1897-99 studied architecture in Caen. 1900 arrived in Paris. 1903 Ecole des Arts Décoratifs, Académie Julian. 1910-11 participated in formation of *Section d'Or* group. 1912 first one-man exhibition Kahnweiler Gallery. 1912-14 reduction of form to cubic volumes and primary colors. World War I increased his awareness of machines; 1917 began Mechanical Period. 1920 met Le Corbusier with whom he worked and traveled. 1924 collaborated on *Ballet Mécanique*. 30's and 40's painting became flatter with undulating rhythms. 1940-45 in the United States where he taught at Yale University and Mills College, Oakland, California. Returned to France after the War. 1949 retrospective Musée National d'Art Moderne, Paris.

59. FERNAND LEGER

Woman in Armchair (La Femme au fauteuil). c. 1912-13
Oil on canvas, 51¼ x 38¼"
Unsigned

PROVENANCE:

Daniel-Henry Kahnweiler, Paris
Alphonse Kann, Paris
Mary Callery, New York
Earl L. Stendahl, Hollywood, California, c. 1945
Winston Collection, 1950

EXHIBITIONS:

Cranbrook, 1951, no. 26, ill.
The Art Institute of Chicago, April 12-May 17, 1953, *Léger,* no. 8, p. 84, ill. p. 18. In collaboration with The San Francisco Museum of Art, June 12-August 30, 1953 and The Museum of Modern Art, New York, October 20, 1953- January 3, 1954
University of Michigan, 1955, p. 12, no. 33
D.I.A., 1957-58, no. 61, p. 57, ill. p. 59
D.I.A., 1972-73

REFERENCES:

Tériade, E., *Fernand Léger,* Cahiers d'Art, Paris, 1928, ill. p. 16
Vassar Alumnae Magazine, 1958, ill. p. 12
Delevay, Robert L., *Léger,* Skira, Paris, 1962, p. 48, ill. p. 46
Parker, Clifford S. and Paul L. Grigaut, *Initiation à la culture française,* 1963, second edition, p. xiii, pl. opp. p. 191
Taylor, *Collections,* 1963, p. 292, ill. opp. p. 302
Baro, *Art in America.* 1967, p. 72
Meisel, *The Connoiseur,* 1968, ill. p. 259

W-76

60. FERNAND LEGER

Still Life. 1921
Pencil on paper, 15 x 10″
l.r. "F. L/21"

PROVENANCE:

Curt Valentin Gallery, New York
Winston Collection, 1952

EXHIBITIONS:

University of Michigan, 1955, no. 34, p. 13
D.I.A., 1957-58, no. 62, p. 57, ill. p. 60
D.I.A., 1962, *French Drawings and Watercolors*
Indiana University, *Reflection,* 1971, no. 85, p. 60, ill. p. 66
D.I.A., 1972-73

REFERENCE:

Baro, *Art in America,* 1967, ill. p. 74

G-162

El (Eleazer) Lissitzky 1890-1941

Born Polshinok, Smolensk, Russia. 1909-14 studied at Darmstadt, school of engineering and architecture. 1914 went to Moscow. 1916 showed at *Knave of Diamonds* exhibition, Moscow. 1919 professor at Vitebsk School of Art. Met Malevich; painted first *Proun,* his name for non-objective paintings. 1922 installed *Proun* room according to Constructivist principles at *Grosser Berliner Kunstaustellung,* Russian exhibition in Berlin. Contact with Bauhaus group. 1925 returned to Moscow. 1928 married Sophie Küpers. 1931 appointed permanent chief designer of the Permanent Building Exhibition, Moscow. Designed many exhibition rooms before and after this appointment.

61. EL LISSITZKY

Proun No. 95. c. 1920-23
Oil, collage and gouache on paper, 23⅛ x 19¹/₁₆″
On reverse u.c. "Proun / #95"

PROVENANCE:

Katherine S. Dreier, West Redding, Connecticut
The Pinacotheca Gallery, New York
Winston Collection, 1949

EXHIBITIONS:

Brooklyn Museum, New York, November 19, 1926-January 1, 1927, *International Exhibition of Modern Art,* assembled by the Société Anonyme, no. 199
The Pinacotheca Gallery, New York, October 6-31, 1949, *El Lissitzky,* no. 2
Cranbrook, 1951, no. 28
Rose Fried Gallery, New York, January 16-February 23, 1952, *Coincidences,* no. 10
University of Michigan, 1955, no. 36, p. 13
Contemporary Arts Museum, Houston, February 27-March 24, 1957, *The Sphere of Mondrian,* n. p.
D.I.A., 1957-58, no. 63, p. 60, ill. p. 31
Albright-Knox Art Gallery, Buffalo, March 3-April 14, 1968, *Plus By Minus: Today's Half-Century,* no. 82
D.I.A., 1972-73

REFERENCES:

M. G., *Art News,* vol. 48, no. 7, November 1949, p. 51
American Abstract Artists, ed., *The World of Abstract Art,* 1956, ill. p. 89
Degand and Arp, *Aujourd'hui,* 1957, ill. p. 30
"The Winston Collection on Tour," *Arts,* 1958, ill. p. 36
Seuphor, *Abstract Painting,* 1962, no. 88, p. 308, ill. p. 74

W-81

Morris Louis 1912-1962

Born Morris Bernstein in Baltimore. 1929-33 studied at Maryland Institute, Baltimore. Lived in Baltimore until 1949. 1952-56 taught at Workshop Center for the Arts, Washington, D.C. Style influenced by Helen Frankenthaler's "stain" painting, *Mountains and Sea,* 1952. "Veil" paintings of 1954 and 58-59 are important examples of his personal idiom. Lived in Washington, D.C. until death.

Quo Numine Lasso. 1959

Mixed media on cotton duck, 103 x 77″

l.l. "Louis '59"

PROVENANCE:

Galerie Lawrence, Paris
Winston Collection, 1964

EXHIBITIONS:

Institute of Contemporary Arts, London, Spring 1960, *Morris Louis*
Galerie Neufville, Paris, March 17-April 22, 1961, *Morris Louis*
Galerie Alfred Schmela, Düsseldorf, April 27-May 24, 1962, *Morris Louis*
Galerie Lawrence, Paris, November 9-December 3, 1963, *Morris Louis*
D.I.A., 1969, *Detroit Collects,* no. 99

REFERENCE:

Baro, *Art in America,* 1967, ill. p. 72

W-221

The title for this veil painting was chosen by Clement Greenberg, taken from the first book of Virgil's Aeneid—"What Diety Offended..."

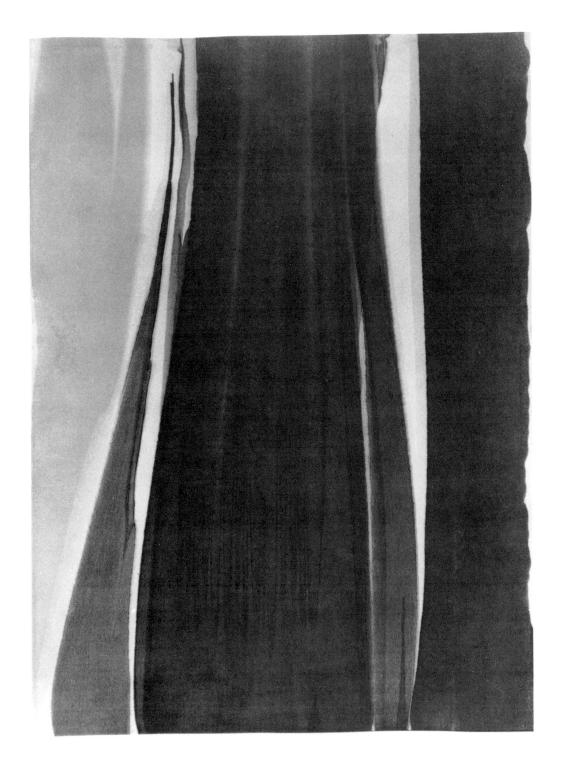

63. MORRIS LOUIS

Late Flowering. 1962
Acrylic resin on unsized duck, 86 x 31½″
On reverse u.c. "Louis 1962"

PROVENANCE:

the artist
Galerie Lawrence, Paris, 1962
Winston Collection, 1964

EXHIBITION:

Galerie Lawrence, Paris, November 9-December 3, 1962,
Morris Louis

W-222

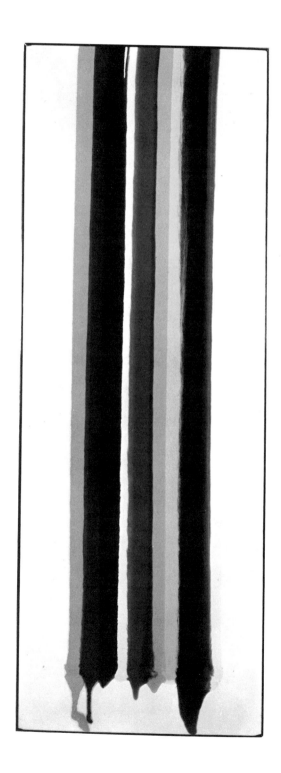

Stanton MacDonald-Wright 1890-1973

Born Charlottesville, Virginia. 1904-05 studied at Art Students' League, Los Angeles. 1907 to Paris to study art. Met Morgan Russell c. 1910. Studied color with Tudor-Hart, read color theories of Chevreul. Devised Synchromy, which emphasized color in reaction to monochromatic Cubism. First Synchromist exhibition *Neue Kunst Salon,* Munich, 1913. 1916-18 lived in New York, exhibited at Steiglitz' *291.* 1919 produced first full-length stop motion color film. Developed color process for movies. 1920 interest in Oriental philosophies; 1924 returned to representation under influence of Chinese painting. Active as teacher and writer. From 1954 both non-objective and figurative work. Repeated visits to Orient. Lived in California and Tokyo.

Conception Synchromy; Conception; Arm Organization
1916-17?
Oil on canvas mounted on cardboard, 29¾ x 11⅛″
l.l. "S.M.W."

PROVENANCE:

the artist, Paris
Winston Collection, 1956

EXHIBITIONS:

La Galerie Arnaud, Paris, April 12-25, 1956, *MacDonald-Wright,* no. 19 (ill. on catalogue cover is for larger painting formerly in the Earl L. Stendahl Collection, Hollywood, California)
D.I.A., 1957-58, no. 64, p. 60, ill. p. 61
D.I.A., 1962, *American Drawings and Watercolors,* no. 178, p. 11
The Corcoran Gallery of Art, Washington, D.C., April 26-June 2, 1963, *The New Tradition—Modern Americans before 1940,* no. 67, p. 62, ill. p. 25
The Baltimore Museum of Art, October 6-November 15, 1964, *1914: An Exhibition of Paintings, Drawings, and Sculpture,* no. 136, p. 89
M. Knoedler & Co., Inc. New York, October 12-November 6, 1965, *Synchromism and Color Principles in American Painting: 1910-1930,* no. 34, pp. 27, 51
The Solomon R. Guggenheim Museum, New York, June 23-October 23, 1966, *Gauguin and the Decorative Style*
National Collection of Fine Arts, Smithsonian Institution, Washington, D.C., May 4-June 18, 1967, *The Art of Stanton MacDonald-Wright,* no. 5, p. 27
The U.C.L.A. Art Galleries, Los Angeles, November 16-December 20, 1970, *Stanton MacDonald-Wright: A Retrospective Exhibition, 1911-1970,* no. 6, ill.
D.I.A., 1972-73

REFERENCES:

Seuphor, Michel, *L'Art abstrait: ses origines, ses premiers maîtres,* Paris, 1950, ill. p. 155 (ill. of Stendahl painting)
Seuphor, Michel, *Dictionnaire de la peinture abstraite,* Hazan, Paris, 1957, p. 20 (Translated into English by Lionel Izod, John Montague and Frances Scarfe, *Dictionary of Abstract Painting,* Paris Book Center, New York)
"A Splendor of Springtime Shows," *Time,* vol. LXXXI, no. 19, May 10, 1963, ill. p. 62
Seuphor, Michel, *L'Art abstrait: vol. 1: 1910-1918, origines et premiers maîtres,* Maeght, Paris, 1971, no. 51, p. 216, ill. p. 115 (ill. for Stendahl painting) (hereafter cited as Seuphor, *L'Art abstrait,* 1971)

W-94

Although this painting has often been dated c. 1914, the
1916-17 date attributed to it by William Agee seems more
probable. (Agee, Knoedler catalogue, 1965, p. 51) It is a
smaller version of the very similar 1916 painting formerly
in the collection of Earl L. Stendahl, Hollywood, California,
(current whereabouts unknown); that fact alone increases
the likelihood of the accuracy of the later date.

André Masson b. 1896

Born in Balagny, France. Studied art at Académie Royale des Beaux Arts, Brussels; 1912 at Ecole des Beaux Arts, Paris under Baudouin. 1917 wounded in World War I severely, psychologically as well as physically. Paintings of early 20's influenced by Cubism. Among the first Surrealists. 1925 regularly contributed automatic drawings to *La Révolution Surréaliste*. 1934-36 lived in Spain. Late 30's turned to figurative Surrealism influenced by Picasso. 1941-45 to United States; this period marked by automatist, expressionist approach. Returned to France 1945, painted in more expressionist manner. Throughout career created many scenic designs. Important in linking American Abstract Expressionism and European Surrealism.

65. ANDRE MASSON

Nude under Fig Tree. 1944
Charcoal and ink on paper, 23¹³⁄₁₆ x 18″
Signed l.l. "André Masson"

PROVENANCE:

Buchholz Gallery, New York
Winston Collection, 1946

EXHIBITIONS:

D.I.A., 1947, *A Loan Exhibition of French Painting, XVII-XX Centuries*, p. 6
Cranbrook, 1951, no. 69
University of Michigan, 1955, no. 41, p. 13, ill.
D.I.A., 1957-58, no. 67, p. 61, ill. p. 62
D.I.A., 1962, *French Drawings and Watercolors*
Indiana University, 1971, *Reflection*, no. 98, pp. 18, 65, ill. p. 17

REFERENCE:

Reynolds, Graham, *Twentieth Century Drawings*, London, 1946, no. 63, ill.

G-165

Henri Matisse 1869-1954

Born at Le Cateau, France. Studied law 1887-88. 1892 studied
at Académie Julian, Paris, under Bouguereau and Ferrier;
1893 at Ecole des Beaux Arts, Paris, under Moreau. 1893
visited Provence and came under influence of Cézanne. 1899
worked at atelier of Carrière; began experiments in sculpture. Although primarily a painter, continued to sculpt
throughout his career, influential as a sculptor. 1904 after
brief Pointillist period turned to use of pure, flat color. 1905,
with Derain, Marquet, Vlaminck and others, formed *Fauve*
group, notable for use of brilliant, arbitrary color and direct
brushwork. 1911-13 visits to Morocco: oriental color influence, exotic landscapes. 1913 influence of Cubism. 1917
settled in Nice. Early 1920's period of *Odalisques* marked
by use of sensuous color and pattern; strong three-
dimensionality in 1920's. 1930 travelled in Europe, Russia,
Oceania, United States where he painted murals for Dr.
Barnes. 1930's characterized by linearism. 1936 retrospec-
tives, Paris, New York, Stockholm. 1939 settled in Vence,
produced many collages. 1949 began decoration of Domini-
can Chapel, Vence. 1950's numerous compositions of
colored, cut paper.

66. HENRI MATISSE

The Velvet Gown (Robe de velours). 1936
Ink on paper, 14½ x 19⅜"
l.l. "Henri-Matisse 36"

PROVENANCE:

the artist, Paris
Pierre Matisse Gallery, New York, c. 1937
Winston Collection, 1948

EXHIBITIONS:

Pierre Matisse Gallery, New York, Summer 1939, *Summer Exhibition French Modern*
Cranbrook, 1951, no. 70
University of Michigan, 1955, no. 42, p. 13, ill.
D.I.A., 1957-58, no. 68, p. 61. Did not travel
Indiana University, 1971, *Reflection*, no. 100, p. 66, ill. p. 70

G-174

Jean Metzinger 1883-1956

Born in Nantes. 1898 began to paint; settled in Paris; attended many academies but was dissatisfied with all of them. 1903-08 work influenced first by Neo-Impressionists, then Fauves. 1909 exhibited at *Salon des Indépendants* and with the *Section d'Or*. 1912 published *Du Cubisme* with Albert Gleizes, first theoretical work on the movement. Continued to work in the Cubist idiom until his death.

67. JEAN METZINGER
Still Life with Pears. 1912-1917
Oil on canvas, 45¾ x 32″
l.r. "J. Metzinger"

PROVENANCE:

the artist
Léonce Rosenberg, Paris
Galerie La Gentilhommière, Paris
Winston Collection, 1953

EXHIBITIONS:

University of Michigan, 1955, no. 43, ill. p. 14
D.I.A., 1957-58, no. 69, p. 60, ill. p. 63

W-151

Joan Miró b. 1893

Born in Barcelona. 1907-15 intermittent attendance at various art schools. 1918 first one-man exhibition, Barcelona. 1920 moved to Paris, summered at parents' farm in Montroig, Spain. 1920 first participation in Dada activities. Joined Surrealist group 1924. 1925 major one-man exhibition Galerie Pierre, Paris. Use of imaginary and dream imagery encouraged by friendship with Arp and Masson and acquaintance with Klee's work. Around 1940 more rhythmically patterned compositions appeared; 1950's and 60's a gestural idiom of expressive calligraphy developed; 1950's more concentrated work in ceramics and sculpture. Resides in Palma de Mallorca.

Personage; The Brothers Fratellini. 1927
Oil on canvas, 51¼ x 38″
l.c. "Miró/1927"

PROVENANCE:

the artist, Paris
Pierre Loeb, Paris
Pierre Chadourne, Paris
Theodore Schempp & Co., New York
Winston Collection, 1952

EXHIBITIONS:

University of Michigan, 1955, no. 45, p. 14
D.I.A., 1957-58, no. 73, p. 64, ill. opposite title page
The Museum of Modern Art, New York, March 18-May 10, 1959, *Joan Miró,* p. 51, ill. Did not travel
D.I.A., 1972-73

REFERENCES:

Saarinen, *Art News,* 1957, ill. on cover and p. 5
Rubin, William, "Miró in Retrospect," *Art International,* vol. III, nos. 5-6, 1959, ill. p. 37
Dupin, Jacques, *Joan Miró, Life and Work,* Abrams, New York, 1962, no. 190, pp. 166, 168, ill. p. 516
Rubin, William, "Arshile Gorky, Surrealism, and the New American Painting," *Art International,* vol. VII, no. 3, February 1963, ill. p. 36. (reprinted in *New York Painting and Sculpture: 1940-1970,* Dutton, New York, 1969, in association with The Metropolitan Museum of Art, ill. p. 399)
Taylor, *Collections,* 1963, ill. p. 303
Baro, *Art in America,* 1967, ill. p. 72
Miesel, *The Connoisseur,* 1968, p. 262

W-80

According to Dupin, this canvas and a very similar one of the same year, *Three Personages* (or *The Fratellini)* in the Gallatin Collection of the Philadelphia Museum of Art, are "good examples of Miró's most subjective vein of humor." (p. 166) He also explains that Miró gave precise titles to only a few of his paintings, preferring to designate them merely as *Peinture* or *Painting.* Apparently neither of these two works were given the Fratellini title by the artist. Undoubtedly it was someone in Miró's circle at the time—possibly one of the Surrealist poets like Robert Desnos or Paul Eluard—who gave the painting this title. Fratellini refers to the family of circus acrobats and clowns who were very popular in Paris at that time; the title seems appropriate in terms of several other works he made that year which evolved around a circus theme.

Composition in Black and White with Blue Square. 1935
Oil on canvas, 28 x 27⅛"
l.c. "PM 35"

PROVENANCE:

the artist
George L. K. Morris, Paris, 1936
The Pinacotheca Gallery, New York, 1947
Winston Collection, July 1947

EXHIBITIONS:

Museum of Living Art, New York University, 1937, *Piet Mondrian*
Mortimer Brandt Gallery, New York, 1942, *American Abstract Artists Exhibition*
The Museum of Modern Art, New York, March 21-May 13 1945, *Piet Mondrian*
Cranbrook, 1951, no. 36, ill.
University of Michigan, 1955, no. 48, p. 14
D.I.A., 1957-58, no. 76, p. 64, ill. p. 66
D.I.A., 1969, *Detroit Collects,* no. 121
D.I.A., 1972-73

REFERENCES:

Seuphor, Michel, *Piet Mondrian: Life and Work,* Abrams, New York, 1956, no. 538, p. 37, ill. p. 69
Neumayer, Alfred, *Die Kunst in unserer Zeit: Versuch einer Deutung,* Henry Goverts, Stuttgart, 1961, no. 16, p. 119, p. 174. (Published in English as *The Search for Meaning in Modern Art,* 1964, ill. p. 93, pl. xxiv)
Seuphor, *Abstract Painting,* 1962, no. 150, p. 310, ill. p. 110
Busignani, Alberto, *Mondrian,* Arts et Métiers Graphiques, Paris, 1968, p. 37, ill. p. 69
Elgar, Frank, *Piet Mondrian,* Praeger, New York, 1968, no. 150, ill. p. 161
Hakanson, Joy, " 'Detroit Collects' — but not from Michigan," *The Detroit News,* May 25, 1969, ill. p. 2-E
Tomassoni, Italo, *Mondrian,* 1970, no. 39, ill.
Akane, Kazuo, *Piet Mondrian — Life and Art,* 1971, no. 78, ill. (in Japanese)

W-71

Piet Mondrian 1872-1944

Born in Amersfoort, The Netherlands. 1892-97 studied at Amsterdam Academy of Fine Arts. 1911 saw Cubist works by Braque and Picasso. 1912 moved to Paris. By 1913 style had developed beyond Cubism to a more radical abstraction. Detained in The Netherlands during World War I. 1917 arrived at mature style of vertical and horizontal dissecting lines and flat color planes. 1919 contributed essays to first issue of *De Stijl* periodical; 1918 signed *De Stijl* manifesto. 1919 returned to Paris. 1930 exhibited with *Cercle et Carré.* 1931 joined *Abstraction-Création* group. 1938 World War II forced him to London. 1940 moved to New York. Influenced by the vitality of New York and began to develop more dynamic, less classical style.

Henry Moore b. 1898

Born in Castleford, Yorkshire, England. 1919-21 scholarship Leeds School of Art and Royal College of Art, London, where he taught until 1931. Impressed by Egyptian, Etruscan, Mexican and African sculpture at British Museum. 1924 first reclining figure. 1930 sculpture becomes more abstract and organic. 1936 founding member of English Surrealist Group; exhibited *International Surrealist Exhibition,* London. 1928 first one-man exhibition. 1943 first one-man exhibition in New York. 1948 International Sculpture Prize, Venice Biennale. 1957 reclining figure for UNESCO Headquarters, Paris. 1963-64 two-piece reclining figure, Lincoln Center, New York.

70. HENRY MOORE

Abstract Sculpture. 1937
Hoptonwood stone, 19¾ x 17¼ x 13¾″
Unsigned
Unique piece

PROVENANCE:

the artist
Curt Valentin, New York
Martha Jackson Gallery, New York, 1955
M. Knoedler & Co., New York, August 1959
Winston Collection, October 1959

EXHIBITION:

Museum Boymans van-Beuningen, Rotterdam, May 30-July 12, 1953, *Henry Moore,* no. 12, ill.

REFERENCES:

Sweeney, James Johnson, *Henry Moore,* The Museum of Modern Art, New York, 1946, ill. p. 45
Read, Herbert, ed., *Henry Moore Sculpture and Drawings,* 1949, 3rd revised and enlarged edition, pl. 54
Giedion-Welcker, Carola, *Contemporary Sculpture,* 1955, ill. pp. 130, 131; revised edition, 1960, ill. pp. 144, 145
Sylvester, Robert, ed., *Henry Moore Sculpture and Drawings,* 1957, 4th edition, no. 179, p. 11, ill. p. 106
Taylor, *Collections,* 1963, ill. p. 298
Read, Herbert, *Henry Moore, A Study of His Life and Work,* Praeger, New York, 1966, no. 92, p. 114, ill. p. 114

W-54

Kenneth Noland b. 1924

Born in Ashville, North Carolina. 1946-48 studied with Ilya
Bolotowsky at Black Mountain College. 1948-49 studied
with Zadkine in Paris. Taught at Institute of Contemporary
Art, Washington, D.C. and Catholic University. 1953 went to
Helen Frankenthaler's studio with Morris Louis where he
was introduced to the "stain" technique. 1957-58 first one-
man show at Tibor de Nagy Gallery, New York. Stylistic
development from "pin wheels" to "bulls eyes" to elliptical
"tiger's eyes"; 1962 began chevrons, then diamonds and finally horizontal bands of color. Fall 1967 taught at Bennington College, Vermont. Lives and works in New York City.

71. KENNETH NOLAND

Baba Yagga. 1964.
Acrylic resin on unsized canvas, 64 x 66¼″
On reverse, vertically "Baba Yagga/1964/Kenneth Noland"

PROVENANCE:

the artist
André Emmerich Gallery, New York
Winston Collection, 1964

EXHIBITION:

André Emmerich Gallery, New York, November 10-28,
1964, *Kenenth Noland*

W-223

Clement Greenberg explained to Lydia Winston Malbin in a
letter dated July 20, 1964, that the title means in Serbian
"benign sorceress" or a "good witch."

Eduardo Paolozzi b. 1924

Born in Edinburgh, Scotland. 1943 studied at Edinburgh College of Art; 1944 Slade School of Art, London. 1947 first one-man exhibition at Mayer Gallery, London. 1947-50 worked in Paris. Exhibited work at Galerie Maeght with group *Les mains éblouie*. Influenced by Dada and Surrealism. Sculptures present anguished images of modern man, using cast-off objects assembled within a human framework. 1950 began work in graphics. 1950-54 worked on several architectural projects. 1955-58 taught at St. Martin's School of Art, London. Work after 1961 composed of simply structured monumental components, assembled with technological precision.

Head. 1957

Bronze, 38½ x 26½″

Back, base "Paolozzi"

Unique piece

PROVENANCE:

Betty Parsons Gallery, New York
Winston Collection, 1961

EXHIBITIONS:

Hanover Gallery, London, November 11-December 31, 1958, *Paolozzi Sculpture,* no. 4, ill. p. 6
Palazzo Grassi, Venice, 1959-60, *Vitalità nell'arte*
Betty Parsons Gallery, New York, March 14-April 2, 1960, *Paolozzi,* no. 4

REFERENCES:

Alloway, Lawrence, "London Chronicle," *Art International,* vol. II, no. 9-10, 1958-59, ill. p. 58
Taylor, *Collections,* 1963, p. 303
Read, *Modern Sculpture,* 1964, no. 269, p. 234
Kuh, Katherine, *Break-Up: The Core of Modern Art,* New York Graphic Society, Greenwich, 1965, no. 90, p. 136, ill. p. 128
Kirkpatrick, Diane, *Eduardo Paolozzi,* New York Graphic Society, Greenwich, 1971, no. 25, p. 136, ill. p. 36

W-44

Antoine Pevsner 1886-1962

Born in Orel, Russia. Attended School of Fine Arts, Kiev; Academy of Fine Arts, St. Petersburg. 1912, 1913-14 in Paris. 1915-16 in Oslo with younger brother Naum Gabo. 1917 returned to Russia and taught at Moscow Academy of Fine Arts with Kandinsky and Malevich. 1920 wrote *Realist Manifesto* with Gabo expressing a revolutionary esthetic for sculpture as space and void, incorporating the dimension of time. 1923 moved to Paris. 1930 became French citizen. 1931 joined *Abstraction-Création;* 1946 co-founder of group *Réalités Nouvelles.* 1948 large retrospective at The Museum of Modern Art, New York with Gabo. 1957 retrospective at Musée National d'Art Moderne, Paris.

73. ANTOINE PEVSNER

Square Relief. 1922
Painted plastic on cardboard, 21 x 20¾″
l.r. "Pevsner"

PROVENANCE:

Rose Fried Gallery, New York
Winston Collection, 1952

EXHIBITIONS:

Rose Fried Gallery, New York, January 16-February 23, 1952, *Coincidences,* no. 16
D.I.A., 1957-58, no. 77, p. 64
D.I.A., 1972-73

REFERENCE:

Peissi, Pierre and Carola Giedion-Welcker, *Antoine Pevsner,* Griffon, Neuchâtel, Switzerland, 1961, no. 29, p. 148, ill.

W-148

74. ANTOINE PEVSNER

Figure. 1925
Copper, 20½ x 6 x 6″
Front r. base "Pevsner"

PROVENANCE:

Tristan Tzara, Paris
Winston Collection, 1954

EXHIBITIONS:

University of Michigan, 1955, no. 49, p. 14
D.I.A., 1957-58, no. 78, p. 64, ill. p. 67. Did not travel

REFERENCES:

"The Winston Collection on Tour," *Arts,* 1958, ill. p. 39
Peissi, Pierre, and Carola Giedion-Welcker, *Antoine Pevsner,*
Griffon, Neuchâtel, Switzerland, 1961, no. 54, p. 149, ill.
Taylor, *Collections,* 1963, pp. 292, 302
Baro, *Art in America,* 1967, ill. p. 75
Goldwater, *Space and Dream,* 1967, ill. p. 76

W-147

75. ANTOINE PEVSNER

Fresco, Fauna of the Ocean (Fresque, le faune de l'océan).
1944
Brass and oxidized tin, 20¾ x 28″
l.r. "AP 44"

PROVENANCE:

the artist
Winston Collection, 1956

EXHIBITIONS:

The Museum of Modern Art, New York, February 10-April
25, 1948, *Gabo-Pevsner*, p. 82, ill. p. 74
Musée National d'Art Moderne, Paris, December 21, 1956-
March 10, 1957, *Antoine Pevsner*, no. 41, p. 20, pl. XII
D.I.A., 1957-58, no. 79, p. 64, ill. p. 10
D.I.A., 1969, *Detroit Collects*, no. 148
D.I.A., 1972-73

REFERENCES:

Drouin, René, ed., *Antoine Pevsner*, Paris, 1947, ill.
Bernier, Rosamond, "Propos d'une sculpteur," interview with
Pevsner, *L'Oeil,* no. 23, November 1956, ill. pp. 32-33
(Reprinted in English as "Pevsner or Constructivism,"
Aspects of Modern Art: The Selective Eye III, Paris and New
York, 1957, ill. pp. 156-57)
Massat, René, *Antoine Pevsner et le Constructivisme*, Paris,
1956, ill.
Degand and Arp, *Aujourd'hui*, 1957, ill. p. 30
Saarinen, *Art News,* 1957, fig. 3, p. 65, ill. p. 32
Mellquist, *XXe Siècle,* 1958, n.p.
Peissi, Pierre and Carola Giedion-Welcker, *Antoine Pevsner,*
Griffon, Neuchâtel, Switzerland, 1961, no. 95, p. 150, ill.
Taylor, *Collections,* 1963, p. 302, ill. pp. 299, 303
Kuh, Katherine, *Break-Up: The Core of Modern Art,* New
York Graphic Society, Greenwich, 1965, no. 77, pp. 112-13,
136, ill.
Francoeur, *Chicago Mid-West Art,* 1967, ill. p. 7

W-58

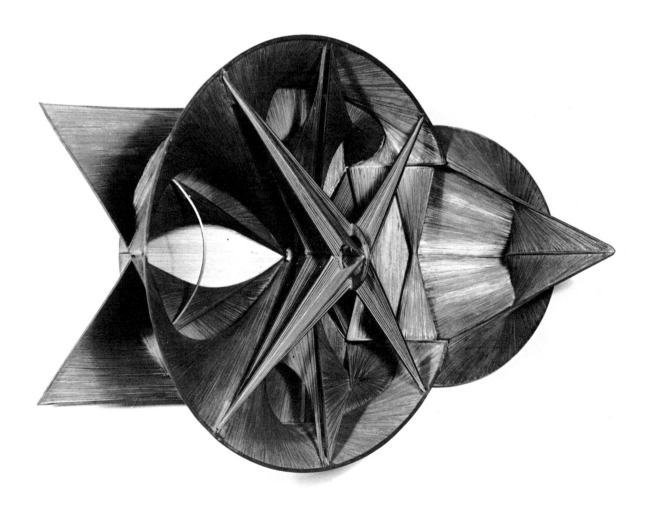

Francis Picabia 1879-1953

Born in Paris of Spanish father and French mother. 1895 entered Ecole des Arts Décoratifs, Paris. Painted in Impressionist style. 1909 began to work in manners related to Fauvism, Cubism, and Abstract art. 1911 met Marcel Duchamp and joined the Puteaux group which became *Section d'Or*. 1913 came to United States for the Armory Show. One-man exhibition at *291*, New York, 1913. 1915 beginning of machinist or mecanomorphic period in which he made imaginary living machines. 1916-21 participated in Dada manifestations and contributed to Dada publications. After 1927 showed in Paris Salons with Surrealists. 1933-39 worked in a variety of styles: simplified naturalistic figures as well as landscapes in Impressionist and Fauvist manners. Retrospective at Galerie René Drouin, 1949. Died in Paris.

Landscape, La Creuse (Paysage de La Creuse). c. 1912
Oil on canvas, 29 x 36½″
l.r. "Picabia"

PROVENANCE:

Gabrielle Buffet-Picabia, Paris
Rose Fried Gallery, New York
Winston Collection, 1952

EXHIBITIONS:

Galerie René Drouin, Paris, March 4-26, 1949, *491, 50 ans de plaisir*, no. 7
Rose Fried Gallery, New York, opened February 15, 1950, *Picabia*, no. 1
Rose Fried Gallery, New York, December 7, 1953-January 8, 1954, *Duchamp and Picabia*, no. 1
University of Michigan, 1955, no. 20, p. 14
D.I.A., 1957-58, no. 80, p. 67, ill. p. 68
The Solomon R. Guggenheim Museum, New York, September 17-December 6, 1970, *Francis Picabia*, no. 21, p. 65, ill. Travelled to Art Gallery of Ontario, Toronto, February 26-April 4, 1971; Detroit Institute of Arts, May 4-June 27, 1971 (hereafter cited as Guggenheim, 1970-71, *Picabia*)
D.I.A., 1972-73

REFERENCES:

Pearlstein, Philip, "The Symbolic Language of Francis Picabia," *Arts*, vol. 30, no. 4, January 1956, ill. p. 41
Buffet-Picabia, Gabrielle, *Aires abstraites*, Pierre Cailler, Geneva, 1957, pp. 26-27
"The Winston Collection on Tour," *Arts*, 1958, ill. p. 36
LeBot, Marc, *Francis Picabia, et la crise des valeurs figuratives, 1900-1925*, Klincksieck, Paris, 1968, no. 41, pp. 99-100 (hereafter cited as LeBot, 1968)
Rubin, William S., *Dada and Surrealist Art*, Abrams, New York, 1969, no. 24, p. 44, ill. p. 45
Seuphor, *L'Art abstrait*, 1971, no. 9, p. 211, ill. p. 20
Tall, William, "Picabia: His Creed, Constant Change," *Detroit Free Press*, June 1971, n.p.

W-146

Although this landscape has often been dated 1908, William Camfield has dated it c. 1912 on stylistic grounds. (See Guggenheim Museum *Picabia* catalogue cited above.)

Mechanical Expression Seen through Our Own Mechanical Expression. 1913
Watercolor on paper, 7⅞ x 6⅛″
l.r. "Picabia 1913"; u.c. "Mechanical Expression Seen / Through Our Own/ Mechanical/ Expression"; c. "New York"; l.c. "NPIERKOWSKA"

PROVENANCE:

Tristan Tzara, Paris
Winston Collection, 1954

EXHIBITIONS:

Modern Gallery, New York, January 5-25, 1916, *Picabia,* no. 15
D.I.A., 1957-58, p. 80. Did not travel
D.I.A., 1962, *French Drawings and Watercolors*

REFERENCES:

"Picabia's Puzzles," *The Christian Science Monitor,* Boston, January 29, 1916
Camfield, William A., "The Machinist Style of Francis Picabia," *The Art Bulletin,* vol. XLVIII, no. 3-4, September-December 1966, p. 313, ill. pp. 4, 318 (hereafter cited as Camfield, *Art Bulletin,* 1966)
Larousse, 1969, no. 1147, p. 367

W-35

Portrait of Marie Laurencin, Four in Hand, c. 1917
Ink and watercolor on board, 22 x 17⅞″
l.r. "Francis Picabia"; u.l. "PORTRAIT DE MARIE LAURENCIN/ FOUR IN HAND"; l.c. "A L'OMBRE D'UN BOCHE"; r.c. "LE FIDELE COCO"; l.r. "IL N'EST PAS DONNE A TOUT LE MONDE/D'ALLER A BARCELONE"; "A MI-VOIX"

PROVENANCE:

Rose Fried Gallery, New York
Winston Collection, 1952

EXHIBITIONS:

Galerie Colette Allendy, Paris, October 18-November 16, 1946, *Picabia,* no. 17
Yale University Art Gallery, New Haven, February 11-

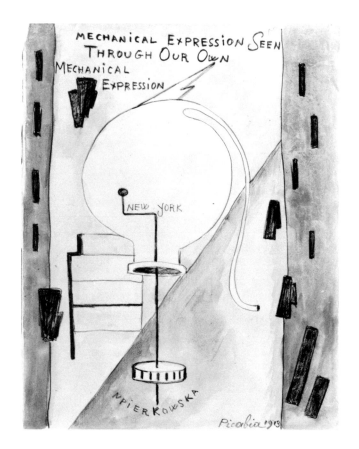

March 11, 1951, and The Baltimore Museum of Art, March 21-April 21, 1951, *Pictures for a Picture: of Gertrude Stein as a Collector and Writer on Art and Artists,* no. 23, p. 33
Rose Fried Gallery, New York, May-June 1951, *Some Areas of Search*
Rose Fried Gallery, New York, January 16-February 23, 1952, *Coincidences*
Rose Fried Gallery, New York, December 7, 1953-January 8, 1954, *Duchamp and Picabia*
University of Michigan, 1955, no. 51, p. 14
D.I.A., 1957-58, no. 81, p. 67, ill. p. 68
Vassar College, 1961, *Centennial Loan Exhibition,* no. 114
D.I.A., 1962, *French Drawings and Watercolors*
Guggenheim, 1963-64, *20th Century Master Drawings,* no. 98
Museum of Modern Art, 1968-69, *The Machine,* ill. p. 88
Guggenheim, 1970-71, *Picabia,* no. 56, p. 101
D.I.A., 1972-73

REFERENCES:

Baur, John I. H., "The Machine and the Subconscious: Dada in America," *Magazine of Art,* vol. 44, no. 6, October 1951, p. 235
Art d'Aujourd'hui, série 4, no. 3-4, May-June 1953, p. 61
Buffet-Picabia, Gabrielle, *Aires abstraites,* 1957, p. 37
Saarinen, *Art News,* 1957, fig. 4, ill. p. 34
"The Winston Collection on Tour," *Arts,* 1958, ill. on cover
Johnson, Una E., *20th Century Drawings, Part I: 1900-1940,* Shorewood, New York, 1964, ill. p. 78
Sanouillet, Michel, *Picabia, l'oeil du temps,* Paris, 1964, p. 102
Camfield, *Art Bulletin,* 1966, pp. 317-18, ill. no. 19
LeBot, 1968, pp. 127-28, ill. no. 41
Larousse, 1969, no. 1078, p. 345
Pearlstein, Philip, "Hello and Goodbye, Francis Picabia," *Art News,* vol. 69, no. 5, September 1970, ill. p. 54
Seuphor, *L'Art abstrait,* 1971, no. 11, p. 211, ill. p. 21

W-43

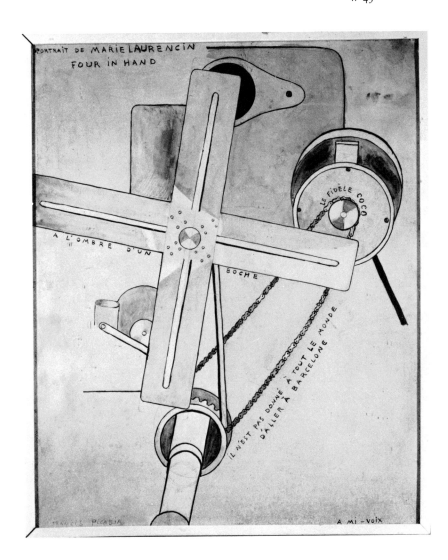

79. FRANCIS PICABIA

Alarm Clock I (Reveil Matin). 1919
Ink on paper, 12½ x 9″
l.l., vertically "Francis Picabia"; l.r. "Reveil Matin"

PROVENANCE:

Tristan Tzara, Paris
Winston Collection, 1954

EXHIBITIONS:

D.I.A., 1957-58, p. 80. Did not travel
D.I.A., 1962, *French Drawings and Watercolors*
Museum of Modern Art, 1968-69, *The Machine,* p. 90, ill.
Guggenheim, 1970-71, *Picabia,* no. 66, p. 109, ill.

REFERENCES:

Tristan Tzara, ed., *Anthology Dada: Dada 4-5,* Zurich,
March 15, 1919, ill. inner cover
Buffet-Picabia, Gabrielle, "Memories of Pre-Dada: Picabia
and Duchamp," Robert Motherwell, ed., *Dada Painters and
Poets,* Wittenborn, New York, 1951, p. 266, ill. p. 130
Arp, Jean, statement in *Picabia in Memoriam,* Orbes, Paris,
April 20, 1955
Verkauf, Willy, *Dada, Monographie einer Bewegung,* M.
Janco and H. Bollinger, 1958, p. 20
Seuphor, *Abstract Painting,* 1962, no. 103, p. 312, ill. p. 81
Carrieri, Raffaele, *Futurism,* Milan, 1964, p. 185, ill. p. 83
Richter, Hans, *Dada: Art and Anti-Art,* McGraw-Hill, New
York and Toronto, 1965, ill. p. 76
Camfield, *Art Bulletin,* 1966, p. 319, ill. no. 27
Musée National d'Art Moderne, Paris, 1966-67, *Dada,* ill. on
front and back of cover
Wescher, Herta, *Collage,* Abrams, New York, 1968, fig. 16,
ill. p. 134

G-171

A similar drawing of approximately the same time is in the
collection of Guido Rossi, Milan. A composition of an alarm
clock, completely hand drawn, unlike this work which was
made by placing inked clock-parts on paper, appears in
Picabia's scrapbook. (See Guggenheim *Picabia* catalogue
cited above).

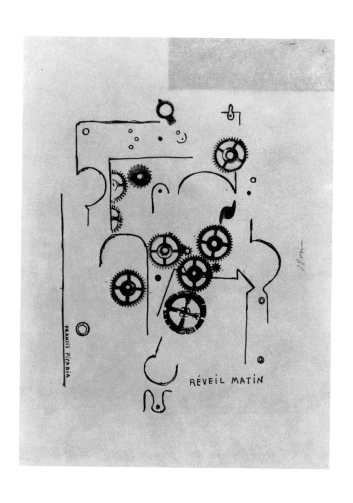

Pablo Picasso 1881-1973

Born in Malaga, Spain. 1891 studied at Da Guarda School of Arts and Industries where father taught. 1895 to Barcelona, entered art school there. 1900 first trip to Paris. 1904 settled in Paris, studio in "Bateau Lavoir." 1901-04 Blue Period; 1904-06 Rose Period. Association with Steins at this time. 1907 influence of African and Iberian art. 1908 association with Braque; with him evolved Analytic, Synthetic Cubism and collage. 1920's neo-classic period. 1925 through 30's marginal Surrealism. 1929-30 produced many sculptures. Late 30's monochromatic and diagrammatic style of *Guernica*. Spent War years in Paris; refused to return to Spain during Franco regime. Intense activity in ceramics and lithography after War. 1948 moved to south of France. Late 40's-50's paintings more loosely constructed. 1963 opening of Picasso Museum, Barcelona. Series of erotic works 1969-70. 1971 major exhibition at Museum of Modern Art, New York, on 90th birthday.

Still Life. 1913
Pencil on paper, 9⅜ x 12³⁄₁₆"
u.r. "Picasso / 1913"

PROVENANCE:

Buchholz Gallery, New York
Winston Collection, 1947

EXHIBITIONS:

Cranbrook, 1951, no. 72
Albion College, 1956, no. 24
D.I.A., 1957-58, no. 82, p. 70, ill. p. 69
D.I.A., 1962, *Picasso*
Marlborough-Gerson Gallery, New York, November-December, 1963, *Artist and Maecenas: A Tribute to Curt Valentin,* no. 176, p. 94, ill.
Fort Worth Art Center Museum and Dallas Museum of Fine Arts, February 8-March 26, 1967, *Picasso Retrospective Exhibitions,* no. 168, p. 102
Indiana University, 1971, *Reflection,* no. 111, pp. 8, 70, ill. p. 8
D.I.A., 1972-73

G-157

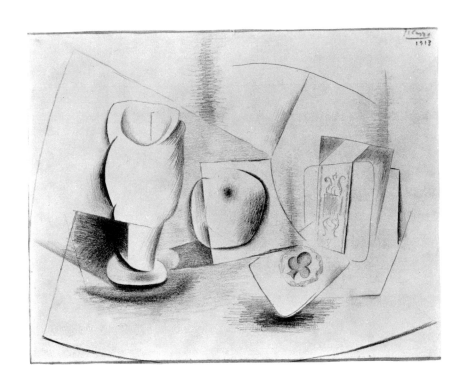

81. PABLO PICASSO

Glass on a Table (Verre sur une table). 1914
Collage, oil, sand and pencil on cardboard
l.r. "Picasso"

PROVENANCE:

Daniel-Henry Kahnweiler, Paris
Jean Lurçat, Paris, 1921
Marthe Hennebert, Paris
Galerie Jeanne Bucher, Paris
Winston Collection, 1952

EXHIBITIONS:

University of Michigan, 1955, no. 53, p. 15
D.I.A., 1957-58, no. 83, p. 70
D.I.A., 1962, *Picasso*
D.I.A., 1972-73

REFERENCE:

Zervos, Christian, *Pablo Picasso, oeuvres de 1912 à 1917*,
Paris, 1942, vol. II, pl. 453, p. 212

W-96

82. PABLO PICASSO

Still Life with Guitar (Guitare sur un table). 1921 recto

The Portal, Fontainbleu (Le Portail). 1921 verso

Oil on canvas, 39 x 38¼"

l.l. recto "Picasso"

PROVENANCE:

the artist, Paris
Pierre Loeb, Paris
Saidenberg Gallery, New York, 1947
Winston Collection, 1953

EXHIBITIONS:

University of Michigan, 1955, no. 54, ill. on cover
D.I.A., 1957-58, no. 84, p. 70, ill. p. 18
D.I.A., 1962, *Picasso*
D.I.A., 1972-73

REFERENCES:

Cahiers d'Art, Paris, nos. 3-10, 1938, ill. for advertisement of
Galerie Pierre, Paris, n.p.
Zervos, Christian, *Pablo Picasso, oeuvres de 1920 à 1922,*
Paris, 1942, vol. IV, pl. 334, p. 128; verso, pl. 282, p. 100
Degand and Arp, *Aujourd'hui,* 1957, ill. p. 30
Vassar Alumnae Magazine, 1958, p. 11
The Bloomfield Art Association, cover for invitation to *The
Arts Festival Ball,* June 11, 1960
Taylor, *Collections,* 1963, p. 303
Baro, *Art in America,* 1967, p. 72
Baro, *The Collector in America,* 1971, p. 183

W-97

83. PABLO PICASSO

Portrait of a Woman Seated under a Light. 1938

Ink and wash on paper, 26 x 17⅛″

l.c. "8.9.38. Picasso"

PROVENANCE:

the artist, Paris
Ronald Emanuel, London, 1938
Charles Fry, London and New York
B. T. Batsford, Ltd., New York
Winston Collection, 1948

EXHIBITIONS:

University of Michigan, 1955, no. 55, p. 15
D.I.A., 1957-58, no. 85, p. 70. Did not travel
D.I.A., 1962, *Picasso*
Indiana University, 1971, *Reflection,* no. 112, p. 71, ill. p. 73
D.I.A., 1972-73

G-189

84. PABLO PICASSO

Portrait of Dora Maar. 1941

Oil on canvas, 16⅛ x 13⅛″

l.l. "Picasso"; on stretcher "25 mi 41"

PROVENANCE:

the artist, Paris
Samuel Kootz, New York
Sidney Janis Gallery, New York, 1947
Winston Collection, 1953

EXHIBITIONS:

University of Michigan, 1955, no. 56, p. 15
D.I.A., 1957-58, no. 86, p. 70, ill. p. 69
D.I.A., 1962, *Picasso*
Fort Worth Art Center Museum and Dallas Museum of
Fine Arts, February 8-March 26, 1967, *Picasso Retrospective
Exhibitions,* no. 64, p. 96
D.I.A., 1972-73

REFERENCES:

Janis, Harriet and Sidney, *Picasso—The Recent Years,* New
York, 1946, pl. 73
Taylor, *Collections,* 1963, p. 293

W-98

Jackson Pollock 1912-1956

Born in Cody, Wyoming. Studied painting at Manual Arts
High School, Los Angeles. 1929 studied with Thomas Hart
Benton, Art Students' League, New York. 1935 settled in
New York. 1938-42 worked on Federal Arts Project. 1943
first one-man show at Peggy Guggenheim's Art of This Century gallery. Before 1947 painted in Surrealist idiom using
mythical or totemic figures. 1947 first paintings in mature
style using drip technique on unprimed canvas. 1950
exhibited at 25th Venice Biennale; was shown extensively in
United States and Europe subsequently. 1956 killed in automobile accident.

85. JACKSON POLLOCK

Moon Vessel. 1945
Oil and enamel on composition board, 33⅜ x 17½"
l.c. "Jackson Pollock"

PROVENANCE:

the artist, New York
Peggy Guggenheim, New York
Winston Collection, 1946

EXHIBITIONS:

Art of This Century, New York, April 2-20, 1946, *Jackson Pollock,* no. 9
University of Michigan, 1955, no. 57, p. 15
D.I.A., 1957-58, no. 88, p. 70, ill. p. 71
D.I.A., 1962, *American Paintings and Watercolors,* no. 183, p. 11
The Museum of Modern Art, New York, April 15-June 4, 1967, *Jackson Pollock,* no. 22, p. 132. Travelled to Los Angeles County Museum of Art, July 19-September 3, 1967
D.I.A., 1969, *Detroit Collects*
D.I.A., 1972-73

REFERENCES:

Saarinen, *Art News,* 1957, p. 64
Taylor, *Collections,* 1963, p. 300
Baro, *Art in America,* 1967, ill. p. 72
Kroll, Jack, "A Magic Life," *Newsweek,* April 17, 1967, ill. p. 97
Miesel, *The Connoisseur,* 1968, fig. 5, ill. p. 262
Baro, *The Collector in America,* 1971, ill. p. 183

W-124

This painting is a fine example of Pollock's style before the post-1947 "drip" work for which he is best known. Clearly he was already preoccupied with a technique incorporating a form of random dripping. Lydia Malbin responded at once to the picture upon seeing it in 1946 at Peggy Guggenheim's gallery, where she had been looking for an André Masson. Pollock's work was completely new to her, but she felt an overwhelming strength in it. She thought there was an affinity between Pollock's largely automatic approach and Masson's automatism. She has speculated on the possible correspondence between the glazed surfaces of her own ceramics and Pollock's surface quality. This painting was the first Pollock purchased by a private collector.

Medardo Rosso 1858-1928

Born in Turin. 1870 to Milan. Drawn to Milanese *Scapigliatura* group. 1882 enrolled in Brera Academy, Milan; expelled 1883. 1884 to Paris, assistant briefly to Dalou; met Rodin. 1886-89 showed at Paris *Salon* and *Salon des Indépendants*. 1900 met Etha Fles who became his patroness. Achieved renown in France and Northern Europe. One man shows: 1904 *Salon d'Automne,* Paris; 1905 Vienna; 1906 London. His concepts derived partially from Impressionism and Symbolism. Greatly admired by Italian Futurists for his rendering of interaction of environment and subject. 1910 first one-man exhibition in Florence; subsequent recognition in Italy aided by Futurist support.

86. MEDARDO ROSSO

The Flesh of Others (Carne altrui; Chair à plaisir; Chair à autrui). 1883
Wax over plaster, 10¾ x 9½ x 6¾″
Unsigned

PROVENANCE:

the artist
Etha Fles
Agatha Verkroost, Amsterdam
Winston Collection, 1963 (through Alexandrine Osterkamp, Amsterdam)

REFERENCES:

Barr, Margaret Scolari, "Medardo Rosso and His Dutch Patroness, Etha Fles," *Nederlands Kunsthistorisch Jaarboek,* V, 13, 1962, ill. p. 241 (hereafter cited as Barr, "Rosso and Etha Fles," 1962)
Barr, Margaret Scolari, *Medardo Rosso,* The Museum of Modern Art, New York, 1963, pp. 23, 25 (hereafter cited as Barr, *Rosso,* 1963)

W-219

87. MEDARDO ROSSO

Man in the Hospital (Malade à l'hôpital; Malato all'
ospedale; Dopo la visita). 1889
Bronze, 9 x 8 x 11″
Unsigned

PROVENANCE:

the artist
Etha Fles
Agatha Verkroost, Amsterdam
Winston Collection, 1963 (through Alexandrine
Osterkamp, Amsterdam)

REFERENCES:

Barr, "Rosso and Etha Fles," 1962, ill. p. 241
Barr, *Rosso,* 1963, p. 30, ill. p. 78
Barr, Margaret Scolari, "Medardo Rosso and His
Utrecht Friend," *Art News Quarterly,* portfolio no. 8,
Spring 1964, p. 81, ill. p. 78 (hereafter cited as Barr,
"Rosso and Friend," 1964)

W-216

While a patient at Lariboisière Hospital in Paris, Rosso was
struck by a sick old man in an armchair who subsequently
inspired this profound image of mute resignation. According
to Etha Fles and Rosso, this piece provided leading sug-
gestions for Rodin's *Monument to Balzac.* Rosso cast this
bronze in Paris.

88. MEDARDO ROSSO

Jewish Boy (Enfant juif; Bimbo ebreo). 1892
Wax over plaster, 8½ x 5 x 8″
Unsigned

PROVENANCE:

the artist
Etha Fles
Agatha Verkroost, Amsterdam
Winston Collection, 1963 (through Alexandrine
Osterkamp, Amsterdam)

REFERENCES:

Barr, "Rosso and Etha Fles," 1962, ill. p. 241
Barr, *Rosso,* 1963, p. 36, ill. p. 78
Barr, "Rosso and Friend," 1964, ill. p. 78

W-218

Rosso, so bent on capturing the transitory and the fragile,
understandably was drawn to children as subjects for his art.
He subtly suggests their vulnerability, intimate dependence
upon their surroundings and their undeveloped individual
potential. Rosso claimed that this sculpture was a likeness
of the young Baron Rothschild.

89. MEDARDO ROSSO

Sick Boy (Enfant malade; Bimbo malato; Bimbo morente). 1893
Wax over plaster, 11¼ x 10 x 7¼"
Unsigned

PROVENANCE:
the artist
Etha Fles
Agatha Verkroost, Amsterdam
Winston Collection, 1963 (through Alexandrine
Osterkamp, Amsterdam)

REFERENCES:
Barr, "Rosso and Etha Fles," 1962, ill. p. 241
Barr, *Rosso,* 1963, pp. 38, 40, ill. p. 78
Barr, "Rosso and Friend," 1964, ill. p. 78

W-217

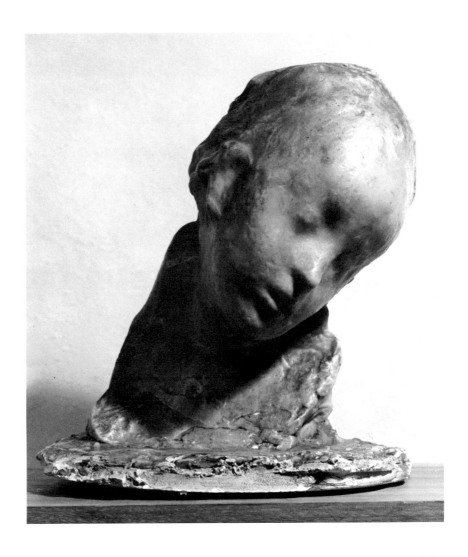

Ecce Puer; Behold the Boy. 1906-07

Wax over plaster, 17 x 14 x 8″

l.c. "M. Rosso"

PROVENANCE:

Anita Gemito, Rome
Peridot Gallery, New York, June 1959
Winston Collection, December 1959

EXHIBITIONS:

Peridot Gallery, New York, December 15, 1959-January 16, 1960, *Medardo Rosso,* no. 12, ill.
D.I.A., 1972-73

REFERENCES:

Ashton, Dore, "A Sculptor of Mystical Feeling," *New York Times,* December 27, 1959, p. x17
Kramer, Hilton, "Medardo Rosso," *Arts Magazine,* December 1959, vol. 34, no. 3, ill. on cover and p. 31
Barr, Margaret Scolari, "Reviving Medardo Rosso," *Art News,* January 1960, vol. 58, no. 9, p. 36, ill. p. 37
"From Exhibitions Here and There," *Art International,* vol. IV, no. 2-3, 1960, no. 5, ill. p. 79
Barr, "Rosso and Etha Fles," 1962, ill. p. 237
Barr, *Rosso,* 1963, pp. 58-59, ill. p. 57
"People Are Talking About Medardo Rosso," *Vogue Magazine,* October 1, 1963, ill. p. 155
Barr, "Rosso and Friend," 1964, p. 81, ill. p. 78
Read, *Modern Sculpture,* 1964, no. 7, pp. 23, 303, ill. p. 20
Geist, Sidney, *Brancusi: A Study of the Sculpture,* Grossman, New York, 1968, ill. p. 184
Baro, *The Collector in America,* ill. p. 182

W-50

This piece, *Man in the Hospital* and *Jewish Boy* were among Rosso's favorite works. In these he believed he had succeeded in transmitting "the emotion, the unification of light, space and air." It is a commissioned portrait of Alfred William Mond, child of Emile Mond of London. Rosso has recorded the boy's sudden appearance from behind a curtain at a large reception in his parents' house. In explanation of the title, Rosso said: "Voilà la vision de pureté dans un monde banal." *Ecce Puer* is the only piece of sculpture Rosso completed during the last quarter of his life.

Morgan Russell 1886-1953

Born in New York. Studied at Art Students' League, New York with Robert Henri, 1906-07. 1909 to Paris, knew Matisse, Leo Stein among others. 1912 developed Synchromism in collaboration with MacDonald-Wright, in which pure color was explored. Influence of Orphism, Delaunay and Kupka important. First Synchromist exhibitions 1913 Munich and Paris; included in Armory Show, New York. After 1920 returned to figurative work. Died in Broomall, Pennsylvania.

Synchromy No. 2, To Light; Synchromy to Light. 1913?
Oil on canvas mounted on cardboard, 13 x 9⅝"
On reverse "1912/No. 2/Morgan Russell"

PROVENANCE:

Rose Fried Gallery, New York
Winston Collection, 1953

EXHIBITIONS:

Galerie Bernheim-Jeune, Paris, October 27-November 8, 1913, *Les Synchromistes: Morgan Russell et Stanton MacDonald-Wright*
Rose Fried Gallery, New York, January 16-February 23, 1952, *Coincidences,* no. 18
Rose Fried Gallery, New York, October 26-November 30, 1953, *Morgan Russell, 1884-1953: An Exhibition in Memoriam,* no. 3
Walker Art Center, Minneapolis, April 1-May 2, 1954, *Morgan Russell: Paintings,* no. 3, ill.
University of Michigan, 1955, no. 58, p. 15
Pioneers of American Abstract Art, circulated by the American Federation of Arts to Atlanta Public Library, December 1-22, 1955; Louisiana State Exhibit Museum, Shreveport, January 4-25, 1956; J. B. Speed Art Museum, Louisville, February 8-March 1; Lawrence Museum, Williamstown, Massachusetts, April 19-May 10; George Thomas Hunter Gallery, Chattanooga, May 24-June 14; Rose Fried Gallery, New York, December 19, 1956-January 9, 1957; no. 32, p. 11
D.I.A., 1957-58, no. 89, p. 70, ill. p. 71
D.I.A., 1962, *American Paintings and Drawings,* no. 142, p. 10
Corcoran Gallery of Art, Washington, D.C., April 26-June 2, 1963, *The New Tradition—Modern Americans before 1940,* no. 83, p. 64
M. Knoedler & Co., Inc., New York, October 12-November 6, 1965, *Synchromism and Color Principles in American Painting,* no. 44, pp. 20, 52, ill. p. 25, fig. 9
National Collection of Fine Arts, Smithsonian Institution, Washington, D.C., December 2, 1965-January 9, 1966, *Roots of Abstract Art in America, 1910-1930,* no. 143
The New Jersey State Museum Cultural Center, Trenton, May 20-September 10, 1967, *Focus on Light,* no. 87
D.I.A., 1972-73

REFERENCES:

Read, *Modern Painting,* 1959, no. 33, p. 365, ill. p. 294
Baro, *The Collector in America,* 1971, p. 187

W-126

William Agee dates the painting 1913 and titles it
Synchromie en bleu-violacé (Synchromy to Light), in spite of
the inscription on the reverse which was probably not
written by the artist. Agee considers it and its sketch
(Collection Los Angeles County Museum of Art) to be
Russell's first completely abstract paintings, which must
have been done in the summer of 1913. "This painting and
the sketch originally carried the French titles, coming to be
known as *Synchromy to Light* by virtue of the passage
from Genesis following the title in the Catalogue of the
Bernheim-Jeune exhibition: *'Alors Dieu dit: Que la lumière
soit! et la lumière fut . . .'* The painting was dedicated
to Mrs. Harry Payne Whitney, Russell's benefactress and
patron from 1908 to 1915. It is probable that this painting is
a later, although identical, version completed in the
early twenties when Russell had returned to his abstract
Synchromies." (Agee, Knoedler catalogue, 1965, p. 52)
Russell himself described this painting: "There is no subject
in the ordinary sense . . . Its subject is the *bleu-foncé*
evolving according to the particular form of my canvas."
(Bernheim-Jeune catalogue, 1913, as quoted from Agee,
Knoedler catalogue, p. 52.)

Luigi Russolo 1885-1947

Born in Portogruaro, near Venice. 1901 to Milan; trained as
a musician, largely self-taught as an artist. Signed Futurist
painting manifestos, 1910. Participated actively in movement
as painter until 1913. From 1913 experiments with Art of
Noises, concerning which he wrote important manifesto.
With painter Ugo Piatti constructed noise producing
machines, *Intonarumori;* 1913-14 gave performances on them
in Italy and England. Participated in later phase of Futurism,
but spent more time in elaborating music than painting.
After 1930 interest in mysticism and Yoga reflected in book
Al di là della materia, 1938. 1940's returned to painting,
but in simple, figurative style.

92. LUIGI RUSSOLO

Nietzsche; Nietzsche and Madness (Nietzsche e la pazzia).

c. 1909

Etching on paper, 8 x 8″ (sheet)

l.l. " 'Nietzsche' "; l.r. "L Russolo"

PROVENANCE:

Benedetta Marinetti, Rome
Winston Collection, 1954

EXHIBITIONS:

Kalamazoo Institute of Arts, 1968, *Graphics from The Winston Collection*
Krannert Art Museum, 1969, *Extensions of the Artist,* p. 29
Toledo Museum of Art, 1972, *A Collector's Portfolio,* no. 133

REFERENCES:

Russolo, Maria Zanovello, *Russolo, l'uomo, l'artista,* Corticelli, Milan, 1958, p. 24
Archivi del divisionismo, vol. 2, no. 2726, p. 221, pl. 587 (another impression)
Martin, 1968, pl. 31 (another impression)

G-274

Russolo apparently left 40 etching plates to his widow, but it is not known how many editions were made of each, either before or after his death.

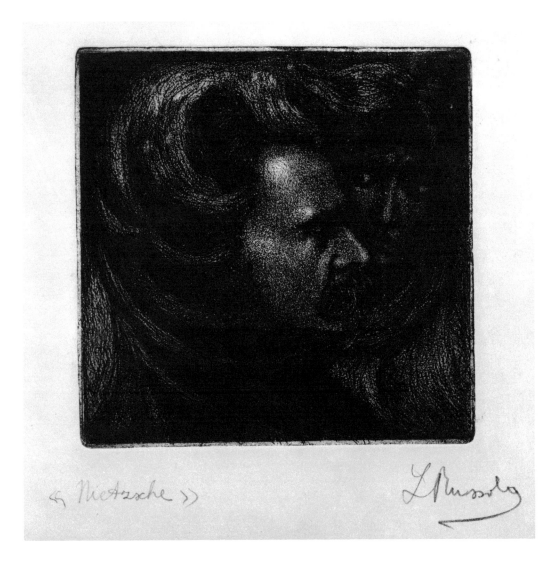

93. LUIGI RUSSOLO

Perfume (Profumo). 1909-10
Oil on canvas, 26⅛ x 25¼"
l.r. "L. Russolo"

PROVENANCE:

Benedetta Marinetti, Rome
Winston Collection, 1956

EXHIBITIONS:

Famiglia Artistica, Milan, opened December 20, 1910, no. 48
Padiglione Ricordi, Milan, opened April 30, 1911, *Prima Esposizione Libera,* sponsored by Società Umanitaria, Casa del Lavoro
D.I.A., 1957-58, p. 80. Did not travel
Museum of Modern Art, 1961, *Futurism,* no. 86, pp. 25, 146, ill. p. 27
D.I.A., 1972-73

REFERENCES:

Russolo, Maria Zanovello, *Russolo, l'uomo, l'artista,* Corticelli, Milan, 1958, pp. 23, 24, 26, 97
Archivi del futurismo, vol. 2, no. 11a, p. 306
Archivi del divisionismo, vol. 2, no. 2729, p. 221, pl. 588
Pierre, José, *Le Futurisme et le dadaisme,* Rencontre, Lausanne, 1967, p. 205, ill. p. 14
Calvesi, Maurizio, "Boccioni e il futurismo milanese," *L'Arte moderna,* vol. V, no. 38, 1967, ill. p. 46
Baro, *Art in America,* 1967, ill. p. 73
Martin, 1968, pp. 83-84, pl. 45
Baro, *The Collector in America,* 1971, ill. p. 181
Tercian, *Le Sédatif qui ne tasse pas,* Printel, Paris, 1972, ill. p. 38

W-12

The synesthetic tendencies which Futurism had inherited from the 19th-century Italian *scapigliatura* and from Symbolism are expressed in this lovely painting. Russolo has created a visual correspondence for non-visual sensations. Form, color and light are arranged to simulate olfactory—and more remotely—auditory sensations and their development in time. The ultra-femininity of this picture has still more in common with the d'Annunzian celebration of the eternal feminine than with the Futurist scorn for women.

Kurt Schwitters 1887-1948

Born in Hanover. 1909-14 studied in Dresden and Berlin.
1918 began experimenting with collage; exhibition at
Der Sturm Gallery, Berlin. 1919 formulated concept of
MERZ, permitting the use of any and all materials for
collages and paintings with collage elements. Throughout
1920's created a construction which he called *Merzbau*
and which grew to fill his home. Considered as a Dada artist
although his works combine Cubist structure with Dada
viewpoint. 1923-32 published *Merz* magazine. 1937-40 lived
in Norway where he began another *Merzbau*. 1941 moved to
England and started a third *Merzbau*.

94. KURT SCHWITTERS

Composition: Ashoff, Ellen. 1922
Collage on paper, 11⅝₁₆ x 8¹³⁄₁₆"
l.r. "Kurt Schwitters, 22"

PROVENANCE:

Tristan Tzara, Paris
Winston Collection, 1954

EXHIBITIONS:

Galerie Berggruen, Paris, June, 1954
Kurt Schwitters Collages, no. 42
University of Michigan, 1955, no. 60, p. 15
Albion College, 1956, no. 25, ill. on cover
D.I.A., 1957-58, no. 93a, p. 73
Indiana University, 1971, *Reflection,* no. 126, p. 77, ill. p. 77

G-62

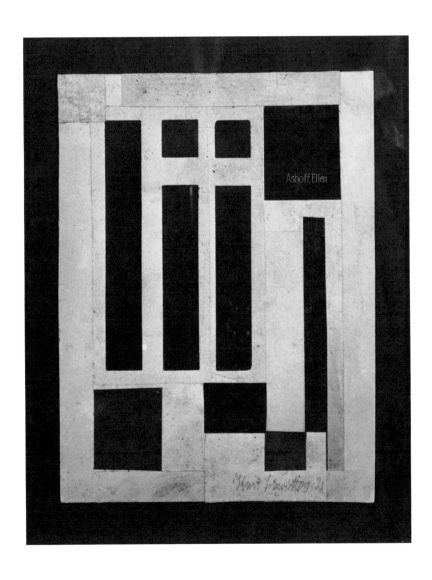

95. KURT SCHWITTERS

C 48 S.Y. Cut Merz. 1946
Collage on paper, 8½ x 6½"
l.c. "KS/46"; l.l. "Kurt Schwitters 1946 Mz F 15";
l.r. "C 46/s y cut"

PROVENANCE:

The Pinacotheca Gallery, New York
Winston Collection, 1948

EXHIBITIONS:

The Pinacotheca Gallery, New York, January 19-February
1948, *Kurt Schwitters*, no. 11
Cranbrook, 1951, no. 44
D.I.A., 1957-58, no. 93c, p. 73, ill. p. 72
Museum of Modern Art, 1961-62, *The Art of Assemblage,*
no. 223, p. 164

W-46

96. KURT SCHWITTERS

S 55 Merz. 1946
Collage and watercolor on paper, 7⁵⁄₁₆ x 5¾″
l.r. "KS/46"

PROVENANCE:

Katherine S. Dreier, West Redding, Connecticut
The Pinacotheca Gallery, New York
Winston Collection, 1948

EXHIBITIONS:

Cranbrook, 1951, no. 43, ill.
University of Michigan, 1955, no. 61, ill. p. 65
D.I.A., 1957-58, no. 93b, p. 73

W-61

97. KURT SCHWITTERS

Ent Garett, Merz. 1947
Collage on paper, 8⅝ x 6⅞"
l.l. "KS 47 Mz F 17"; l.r. "ent garett"

PROVENANCE:

the artist
The Pinacotheca Gallery, New York
Winston Collection, 1948

EXHIBITION:

Cranbrook, 1951, no. 47

W-63

98. KURT SCHWITTERS

Examiner 2861 Merz. 1947

Collage on paper, 8½ x 6⅝"

l.l. "Kurt Schwitters/Examiner 2861"; l.r. "47 100"

PROVENANCE:

the artist
The Pinacotheca Gallery, New York
Winston Collection, 1948

EXHIBITIONS:

Cranbrook, 1951, no. 45
University of Michigan, 1955, no. 62, p. 16
D.I.A., 1957-58, no. 93d, p. 73, ill. p. 72
Indiana University, *Reflection,* 1971, no. 127, p. 77

REFERENCE:

Taylor, *Collections,* 1963, p. 298

W-60

Gino Severini 1883-1966

Born in Cortona, Italy. 1899 to Rome, attended life drawing
classes. 1901 met Boccioni and Balla. 1906 settled in Paris;
associated with avant-garde there. Signed both Futurist
painting manifestos. The most Paris-oriented of the Futurists,
mid-1911 moved into closer contact with Milanese Futurists
whom he familiarized with Parisian developments. 1915-16
turned more toward Cubism and figurative classicism. 1917
one-man exhibition at Stieglitz Gallery, New York. 1921
important treatise, *Du Cubisme au classicisme.*
From 1922 executed many murals. 1940-42 theater décor and
costumes. Lived most of his life in Paris, where he died.

99. GINO SEVERINI

Study for "Portrait of Mme. M.S." 1912
Pastel and charcoal on paper, 19¼ x 13⅞"
l.r. "G. Severini/1912"

PROVENANCE:

the artist
Winston Collection, 1955

EXHIBITIONS:

D.I.A., 1957-58, no. 95, p. 73, ill. p. 74
Museum of Modern Art, 1961, *Futurism*, no. 105, pp. 69, 147
D.I.A., 1972-73

REFERENCES:

Archivi del futurismo, vol. 2, no. 10, p. 338, ill. p. 314
Taylor, *Collections,* 1963, p. 296
Baro, *Art in America,* 1967, ill. p. 73
Baro, *The Collector in America,* 1971, ill. p. 181

W-4

Madame M.S. was the wife of Mr. R. R. Meyer-See,
formerly manager to Martin Henry Colnaghi, then joint
founder and director of the Sackville Gallery and
subsequently owner of the Marlborough Gallery, London.
Severini had his first one-man show at the Marlborough
Gallery in April 1913, but neither this drawing, nor the
related painting (Art Gallery of Ontario, Toronto) were
exhibited then.

100. GINO SEVERINI

*Portrait of Mme. Severini; Portrait of Mlle. Jeanne
Paul Fort.* 1913
Watercolor on paper, 28¾ x 21¼″
l.r. "G. Severini/MCMXIII"

PROVENANCE:

the artist
Winston Collection, 1952

EXHIBITIONS:

Marlborough Gallery, London, April 1913, *The Futurist
Painter Severini Exhibits His Latest Works,* no. 27
Der Sturm, Berlin, Summer 1913, *Gemälde und Zeichnungen
des Futuristen Gino Severini,* no. 27
D.I.A., 1957-58, no. 96, p. 73, ill. p. 24

REFERENCES:

Degand and Arp, *Aujourd'hui,* 1957, ill. p. 31
Mellquist, *XXᵉ Siècle,* 1958, ill., n.p.
Archivi del futurismo, vol. 2, no. 25, p. 338, ill. p. 318
Baro, *The Collector in America,* 1971, ill. p. 181

W-6

Severini's wife is the daughter of the poet Paul Fort, and
this graceful likeness was painted during the months
preceding their marriage which took place on August 28,
1913. Although his Futurist colleagues disapproved of
Severini's bow to convention, Apollinaire, Merrill, and
Marinetti, who arrived from Milan in an appropriate white
automobile, were among the witnesses.

101. GINO SEVERINI

Study for "Sea = Dancer." 1913
Charcoal on paper, 27 7/8 x 19 7/8"
l.r. "G. Severini"

PROVENANCE:

the artist
Winston Collection, 1952

EXHIBITIONS:

University of Michigan, 1955, no. 64, p. 16, ill.
D.I.A., 1957-58, no. 97, p. 73, ill. p. 74
Museum of Modern Art, 1961, *Futurism,* no. 113, p. 147
Guggenheim, 1963-64, *20th Century Master Drawings,*
no. 111

REFERENCES:

Seuphor, *L'Art abstrait,* 1950, p. 153, ill.
Archivi del futurismo, vol. 2, no. 29, p. 338, ill. p. 319
Johnson, Una E., *Twentieth Century Drawings: Part I:
1900-1940,* Shorewood, New York, 1964, pl. 40, p. 72
Seuphor, *Abstract Painting,* 1962, no. 22, p. 315, ill. p. 29
Francoeur, *Chicago Mid-West Art,* 1967, ill. p. 7
Martin, 1968, note 1, p. 145, pl. 102
Baro, *The Collector in America,* 1971, ill. p. 181
Seuphor, *L'Art abstrait,* 1971, no. 40, p. 215, ill. p. 107

G-206

102. GINO SEVERINI

Sea = Dancer; Dancer beside the Sea (Mare = Danzatrice).
1913-14
Oil with sequins on canvas, 36½ x 28¾"
l.r. "G. Severini"; on reverse "Gino Severini/Danseuse aux
Bords de la Mer/à Monsieur et Madame Harry Winston
avec toute ma sympathie Paris 10 -mai -1951 -G. Severini"

PROVENANCE:

the artist
Winston Collection, 1951

EXHIBITIONS:

University of Michigan, 1955, no. 63, p . 16
D.I.A., 1957-58, no. 98, p. 73, ill. p. 75. Did not travel
Museum of Modern Art, 1961, *Futurism*, no. 113, p. 72,
ill. p. 73
D.I.A., 1972-73

REFERENCES:

La Nacion, Buenos Aires, November 9, 1952, p. 1
Vassar Alumnae Magazine, 1958, ill. on cover and p. 1
"The Winston Collection on Tour," *Arts,* 1958, ill. p. 34
Venturi, Lionello, *Gino Severini,* De Luca, Rome, 1961, pl. 29
Archivi del futurismo, vol. 2, no. 38, p. 339, ill. p. 321
Carrieri, Raffaele, *Futurism,* Milione, Milan, 1963, pl. 107
Taylor, *Collections,* 1963, p. 303
Pacini, Piero, *Gino Severini,* Sadea/Sansoni, Florence,
1966, p. 32, pl. 30
Pierre, José, *Le Futurisme et le dadaisme,* Rencontre,
Lausanne, 1967, no. 20, p. 205, ill. p. 24
Calvesi, Maurizio, "I futuristi e la simultaneità: Boccioni,
Carrà, Russolo e Severini," *L'Arte moderna,* vol. V,
no. 39, 1967, ill. p. 102
Martin, 1968, pl. 101, pp. 144-45
Seuphor, *L'Art abstrait,* 1971, no. 5, p. 206, ill. p. 135

W-5

During the winter and spring of 1913, while recuperating
from a severe illness at Anzio, Severini worked on a
number of pictures which he called "plastic analogies."
Sea = Dancer exemplifies stunningly the kind of association
of object-situations that was also described in his
contemporary but unpublished manifesto. He writes, "the
sea with its dance on the spot *(al posto),* its zig-zag
movements and scintillating contrasts of silver and emerald,
in my plastic sensibility evokes the far off vision of a dancer
covered with sparkling paillettes in her surroundings of light,
noises, and sounds." *(Archivi del futurismo,* vol. 1, p. 78)

Sea = Dancer was the first Futurist work to enter the
Winston/Malbin Collection.

103. GINO SEVERINI

Soldier in Trench (Soldati in trincea). c. 1915
Pencil on paper, 7⅜ x 7¾″
l.r. "1914 G Severini" (Inscription added later by artist)

PROVENANCE:

Galerie Berggruen, Paris
Winston Collection, 1956

EXHIBITIONS:

D.I.A., 1957-58, p. 80. Did not travel
Milan, 1960, *Arte Italiana,* no. 176, p. 201, ill. p. 64

G-164

After 1914 Severini began to withdraw from Futurism.
Somewhat unexpectedly, therefore, this gentle artist, who
endured most of the war in his Paris flat, in 1915 produced a
striking series of war paintings. The figure shown here
is related in concept to those found in the masterful
Armored Train, 1915, Collection Mr. Richard S. Zeisler,
New York. But Piero Pacini and Joan M. Lukach agree that
it is preparatory for another unexecuted work in the
same group.

104. GINO SEVERINI

Still Life with Cherries.

Collage on paper, 19½ x 26½″

l.r. "G. Severini"

PROVENANCE:

the artist
Winston Collection, 1952

EXHIBITIONS:

University of Michigan, 1955, no. 65, p. 16
D.I.A., 1957-58, no. 99, p. 73
Museum of Modern Art, *The Art of Assemblage*, no. 227, p. 164, ill. p. 29
Indiana University, 1971, *Reflection*, no. 130, pp. 20, 79, ill. p. 19
D.I.A., 1972-73

G-8

Severini executed a number of fastidiously organized collages with corrugated cardboard such as this one. These have posed considerable problems in dating and are usually assigned to the years of 1912 or 1913 on the basis of dated references within the work. The *Lacerba* page of March 15, 1913 with Papini's provocative heading *"Contro il futurismo,"* found here, could thus be taken as a humorous, contemporary reference to Severini's role in bringing the Florentine writer and his *La Voce* friends into the Futurist fold in 1913. But on stylistic and intellectual grounds the dialogue between Cubism and Futurism suggested in this calm collage is much closer to Severini's approach of 1915 and after. Back in Paris after a prolonged stay in Italy and in close touch with Braque, Picasso and Gris, Severini gradually turned to Cubism. In 1916 Léonce Rosenberg became his dealer and no doubt favored and encouraged the dominantly Cubist control which is found in this collage.

Mario Sironi 1885-1961

Born in Tempio Pausania, Sardinia. To Rome to study mathematics at University, met Severini and Boccioni with whom he visited Balla's studio; decided to become an artist. 1914 first exhibited in Futurist-sponsored show in Rome. Officially joined Futurist movement 1915. Work tended toward personal version of social realism even while member of Futurist group. After World War I style changed; 1920's exhibited with *Novecento* group which sought return to nature, traditional techniques and subjects. Died in Milan.

Composition (Composizione). c. 1913
Crayon and tempera on paper, 18⅞ x 12⅑⁄₁₆″
l.r. "Sironi"

PROVENANCE:

Il Milione, Galleria d'Arte Moderna, Milan
Winston Collection, 1954

EXHIBITIONS:

University of Michigan, 1955, no. 67, p. 16
D.I.A., 1957-58, no. 101, p. 76, ill. p. 77

REFERENCES:

Pica, Agnoldomenico, *Mario Sironi,* Milione, Milan, 1955, ill. p. 9
Scheiwiller, Vanni, ed., *Piccola antologia di poeti futuristi,* Milan, Al Insegna del Pesce, 1958, ill. opposite p. 96
Read, *Modern Painting,* 1959, p. 366, ill. p. 113
Archivi del futurismo, vol. 2, no. 4, p. 390, ill. p. 372
Winston, *Aujourd'hui,* 1962, ill. p. 10
Baro, *The Collector in America,* 1971, ill. p. 181

W-28

The ambivalence of Sironi's loyalities is brought out in this strong, rhythmic drawing. On one hand, the artist leans toward a Cézanne-inspired analysis of solid form similar to that pursued by Léger. On the other, he seeks to suggest in these quasi-automata, the Futurist continuum of motion. Yet the subtle chiaroscuro of this drawing evokes the moonlit unreality of a proto-Dada or *Pittura Metafisica* nightmare.

106. MARIO SIRONI

Man on Motorcycle. 1918
Collage of newspaper and oil on paper, 9¼ x 6¼″
l.r. "Sironi"

PROVENANCE:

Il Milione, Galleria D'Arte Moderna, Milan
Winston Collection, 1951

EXHIBITION:

Indiana University, 1971, *Reflection,* no. 133, p. 80, ill. p. 81

REFERENCE:

Archivi del futurismo, vol. 2, no. 69, p. 392, ill. p. 388

W-32

Frank Stella b. 1936

Born in Malden, Massachusetts. 1950-54 at Phillips Academy, Andover, Massachusetts with Hollis Frampton and Carl Andre; 1954-58 at Princeton, studied there in William Seitz's open painting studio and with Stephen Greene. Early works influenced by Abstract Expressionism and Jasper Johns. Personal style began to emerge with *Black Series*, 1958. 1960 included in *16 Americans* exhibition, the Museum of Modern Art; first one-man exhibition Castelli Gallery, New York. 1961 first trip to Europe. 1964 included in 32nd Venice Biennale; *Shaped Canvas* exhibition at Guggenheim Museum. 1965 trip to Los Angeles; South America. 1967 designed costumes and sets for Merce Cunningham's *Scramble*. 1970 one-man exhibition, Museum of Modern Art, New York.

107. FRANK STELLA

Sketch Red Lead. 1964
Oil on canvas, 55 x 40″, shaped canvas
On stretcher "Sketch Red Lead 1964. F. Stella"

PROVENANCE:

the artist
Galerie Lawrence, Paris, 1964
Winston Collection, 1964

W-227

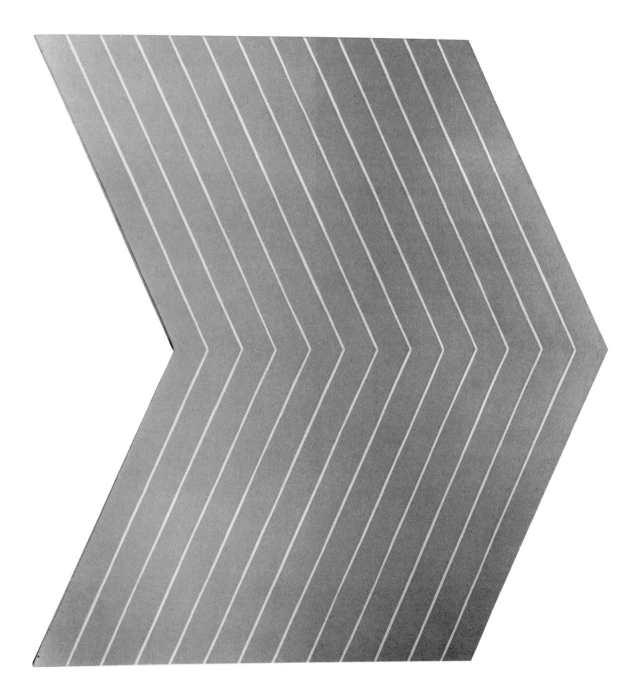

Yves Tanguy 1900-1955

Born in Paris. 1918 joined Merchant Marines and travelled to South America and Africa. 1920 formed lasting friendship with film-maker and poet Jacques Prévert. 1923 started painting, inspired by seeing a work by de Chirico. Painted stark landscapes probably inspired by Brittany where he vacationed as a child. By 1927 had met André Breton and joined Surrealist group, exhibiting with them thereafter. Early 30's after trip to Africa, forms shifted from vegetal to mineral: "boneyard" images, chains of indeterminate beings in infinite landscapes. 1939 upon outbreak of War, to United States. 1940 married American Surrealist, Kay Sage. 1941 moved to Woodbury, Connecticut.

108. YVES TANGUY

Shadow Country (Terre d'ombre). 1927
Oil on canvas, 39 x 31⅝"
l.r. "Yves Tanguy. 27"

PROVENANCE:

Galerie Rive Gauche, Paris
Winston Collection, 1951

EXHIBITIONS:

Cranbrook, 1951, no. 53
University of Michigan, 1955, no. 70, p. 16 ill.
The Museum of Modern Art, New York, September 6-October 30, 1955, *Yves Tanguy—A Retrospective,* ill. p. 25
D.I.A., 1957-58, no. 105, p. 76, ill. p. 80
D.I.A., 1972-73

REFERENCES:

Read, Herbert, *Surrealism,* Harcourt-Brace, London, 1936, pl. 89
Canaday, John, *Mainstreams of Modern Art,* 1959, no. 677, ill. p. 534
Matisse, Pierre, ed., *Yves Tanguy: A Summary of his Work,* New York, 1963, no. 64, ill. p. 60
Goldwater, *Space and Dream,* 1967, ill. p. 77

W-73

Mark Tobey b. 1890

Born in Centerville, Wisconsin. 1906-09 attended Art Institute of Chicago. 1911 to New York. 1917 first one-man exhibition Knoedler Gallery. 1918 converted to Bahá i faith. Met Janet Flanner, Marcel Duchamp. 1922-25 Seattle. 1923 studied Chinese brush painting. 1925-26 travelled to Europe and Near East. 1927-29 lived in Seattle, Chicago, New York. 1931-38 taught in London. 1934 to Orient, studied Japanese calligraphy in Zen monastery. 1935 developed "white writing" of mature style. 1948, chosen for 24th Venice Biennale; 1956 received Guggenheim International Award for *Battle of the Lights;* 1958 first prize 29th Venice Biennale. 1960 to Basel where he still resides. 1961 received first prize Carnegie International, Pittsburgh. 1968 retrospective Dallas Museum of Fine Arts.

Battle of the Lights. 1956
Gouache on paper, 44 x 35½"
l.r. "Tobey / 56"

PROVENANCE:

the artist
Willard Gallery, New York
Winston Collection, 1958

EXHIBITIONS:

The Solomon R. Guggenheim Museum, New York, March 26-June 7, 1957, *Guggenheim International Awards.* Exhibited at Musée National d'Art Moderne, Paris, November 28-December 15, 1956
Museo Nacional des Artes Plasticas, Mexico City, June 6-August 24, 1958, *First Inter-American Biennale Exposition of Painting and Graphic Arts,* sponsored by the Instituto Nacional de Bellas Artes
D.I.A., 1962, *American Paintings and Drawings,* no. 195, p. 11, ill. p. 30
The Museum of Modern Art, New York, September 12-November 4, 1962, *Mark Tobey,* no. 94, p. 109. Travelled to the Art Institute of Chicago, February 22-March 24, 1963

REFERENCES:

Kuh, Katherine, "Mark Tobey: A Moving Encounter," *Saturday Review,* October 27, 1962, p. 30
Tillim, Sidney, "Month in Review," *Arts Magazine,* vol. 37, no. 1, October 1962, ill. p. 51
Baro, *Art in America,* 1967, ill. p. 75

W-49

Joaquín Torres-García 1874-1949

Born in Montevideo, Uruguay. 1891 returned with family to Spain; studied drawing at Escuela de Artes y Oficios and painting with Vinardel. 1892 to Barcelona; studied at Academia de Bellas Artes, Academia Baixas until 1894 or 95. Turn of century style decorative; worked with Gaudí. Met Julio Gonzales in Madrid. 1900 first one-man exhibition at Salon La Vanguardia, Barcelona. 1909-10 travelled to Brussels and Paris. 1911 settled in Spain; 1915 designed first wooden toys. Influence of Futurism, Cubism and dynamism of urban life entered work as more personal style emerged around 1918. 1920 to New York; 1922 to Europe; lived in various countries. 1928 met Van Doesburg; 1929 Mondrian, first Constructivist works. 1930 founded magazine *Cercle et Carré* with Seuphor. 1932 wrote *Raison et nature;* 1934 to Montevideo. 1944 *Universalismo Constructivo* published; founded Torres-García Workshop. His blend of abstraction and representation was extremely influential, particularly in the United States.

110. JOAQUIN TORRES-GARCIA

Symmetrical Composition. 1931

Oil and aqueous paint on canvas, 48 x 24¾"

On reverse u.c. "J. TORRES-GARCIA / MERCEDES 1889-
MONTEVIDEO / "CONSTRUCCION" / COL. M. P."

(frame made by the artist)

PROVENANCE:

Manolita P. de Torres-García, Montevideo
Winston Collection, 1956

EXHIBITIONS:

XXVIII Biennale, Venice, June 16-October 21, 1956, no. 2,
p. 291, ill. no. 94
D.I.A., 1957-58, no. 106, p. 76, ill. p. 78
D.I.A., 1969, *Detroit Collects,* no. 182

REFERENCES:

Degand and Arp, *Aujourd'hui,* 1957, ill. p. 31
Saarinen, *Art News,* 1957, p. 65
"The Winston Collection on Tour," *Arts,* 1958, ill. p. 39
Read, *Modern Painting,* 1959, no. 91, p. 367, ill. p. 303
Miesel, *The Connoisseur,* 1968, fig. 6, ill. p. 262

W-86

Andy Warhol b. 1928?

Born in Cleveland, Ohio. 1945-49 studied pictorial design at Carnegie Institute of Technology (now Carnegie-Mellon University). 1949 settled in New York; worked in commercial design; first commercial work published in *Glamour* magazine. 1957 Art Directors Club Medal for giant shoe advertisement. 1960-61 began paintings with imagery openly derived from comic strips and advertisements. 1963 began making films. Preoccupation with repetition, boredom and, in the mid-60's, with morbid images. Major innovator in novels, cinema, mixed-media fusions of music, film and dance, as well as in graphic art. Lives and works in New York.

Self Portrait. 1966
Acrylic and silkscreen enamel on canvas, 22⅝ x 22⅝"
Unsigned

PROVENANCE:

the artist
Leo Castelli, New York
Winston Collection, 1967

EXHIBITIONS:

University of Michigan, 1969, *Prints from The Collection of Mrs. Lydia Winston Malbin*
Krannert Art Museum, 1969, *Extensions*, p. 31
Pasadena Art Museum, May 12-June 21, 1970, *Andy Warhol.* Travelled to Museum of Contemporary Art, Chicago, July 4-September 6, 1970; Whitney Museum of American Art, May 1- June 20, 1971

REFERENCES:

Lytle, Robert, "Looking For Reality? . . .," *The Michigan Daily,* March 1, 1969, ill.
Glueck, Grace, ". . . Or, Has Andy Warhol Spoiled Success?," *The New York Times,* May 9, 1971, ill. p. 23

W-104

Umberto Boccioni

DRAWINGS AND PRINTS

The following checklist of Boccioni drawings and prints is drawn from Joshua C. Taylor's *The Graphic Work of Umberto Boccioni*, The Museum of Modern Art, New York, 1961. That catalogue lists almost all Boccioni's graphics, and contains all those in the Winston/Malbin Collection. Each entry is marked with the Taylor catalogue number (T-00) and the Winston/Malbin Collection number (W-00). Revisions in dating, grouping and titles have been made by Marianne W. Martin.

DRAWINGS

112. *Young Man on the Bank of a River.* 1902?

Black chalk with traces of red and green chalk with white gouache on buff wove, 11¾ x 8⅝″
l.r. "B 902"(?)
T-1; W-142

Verso: *Study of a Wagnerian Scene (?).* c. 1908

Unsigned
W-321

113. *Study for "Beata Solitudo."* 1907

Pencil on brown wove with blue-gray thread, 13½ x 8¼″
l.r. "Umberto Boccioni/907"
T-18; W-203

Verso: *Summary Sketches.* 1907

Pencil
Unsigned

114. *Study for "Beata Solitudo."* 1907

Pencil, with graffiti in pen and India ink, on white wove, 7⅜ x 4⅝″
l.r. "U Boccioni"
T-19; W-x73E

115. *Pianist and Listener.* c. 1907

Pen and brush with black ink, 7 x 7¼″
l.r. "Boccioni"
T-13; W-162

116. *Standing Nude Girl.* c. 1907

Soft Pencil on ivory bristol board, 16⅝ x 7″
l.r. "Umberto Boccioni"
T-22; W-130

117. *Study of an Arm with Hand Resting on the Shoulder.* c. 1907

Pencil on white wove, 9⅞ x 5¾″
l.r. "Umberto Boccioni"
T-23; W-x63

118. *Study of Two Hands and Forearms.* c. 1907

Pencil on buff wove, 5⅞ x 9⅞″
l.r. "U Boccioni"
T-25; W-x35

119. *Study for "Landscape with Four Peasants at Work."* 1907-08

Pencil on white wove, 4⅝ x 5⅞″
l.r. "UB"
T-6; W-x78

120. *Head of a Bull.* 1907-08

Pencil on white wove, 6¼ x 4⅝″
l.r. "Boccioni"
T-8; W-x46

Verso: *Body of a Bull.* 1907-08

Pencil
l.l. "U. Boccioni"

112

114

116

121. *Study of a Bull's Body.* 1907-08

Pencil on white wove, 4½ x 6⅛"
l.r. "Boccioni"; l.c. "UB"
T-11; W-x4

Verso: *Study of a Bull's Forelegs.* 1907-08
Pencil
Unsigned

122. *Study of a Bull's Forelegs.* 1907-08

Pencil on white laid, 5¼ x 4"
l.r. "UB" / "Boccioni"
T-12; W-x5

Verso: *Sketch of a Bull's Head.* 1907-08
Pencil
Unsigned

123. *Study for "Lombard Landscape: Rural Symphony."* 1908
Pencil on white wove, 4¼ x 6¼"
l.r. "Boccioni"
T-7; W-x1a

Verso: *Woman Seen from the Back; Architectural Detail with Notation.*
Pencil
Unsigned

124. *Study for "Lombard Landscape: Rural Symphony."* 1908

Pencil on white wove, 6⅛ x 4½"
l.r. "Umberto Boccioni"
T-113; W-x24

Verso: *Studies with Script*
Pencil
Unsigned

125. *Study for "Lombard Landscape: Rural Symphony."* 1908

Pencil on white wove, 6⅝ x 4¼"
u.l. "B"; l.r. "Boccioni"
T-114; W-x31

Verso: *Detail of a Tree Trunk*
Pencil
l.r. "Boccioni"

126. *Study of Trees with Two Kneeling Figures and Urn.* c. 1908

Pencil on white wove, 4½ x 6⅞"
l.c. "UB"
T-123; W-x75

127. *Sheet of Studies with Sketch of Window and Foliage, and Study of Arm.* c. 1908

Pen and black ink on white laid, 5⅜ x 7⅞"
l.r. "Boccioni"
T-66; W-x69

117

119

128. *Seated Woman; Study for "The Story of a Seamstress."* 1908

Pencil on buff wove, 7 x 6¾″
l.r. "Umberto Boccioni"
T-33; W-x30

Verso: *Graffiti*

Pencil
Unsigned

129. *Head of a Young Woman; Study for "The Story of a Seamstress."* 1908

Pencil on buff wove, 6½ x 6½″
l.r. "Boccioni"
T-34; W-196

130. *Man Confronting Spectre of a Woman.* c. 1908

Pen and brown ink on buff wove, 7⅞ x 4¼″
l.r. "Boccioni"
T-37; W-x96

Verso: *Sheet of Studies with Figures*

Pen and brown ink
Unsigned

131. *Embracing Couple on a Cloud over a Lake with Floating Heads.* 1908

Pencil, pen, brush with India ink and wash on white wove,
6⅝ x 4¾″
u.r. "Quanto c'è di male nella felicità
T-38; W-x20

132. *Kneeling Man; Study for "The Dream: Paolo and Francesca."* 1908

Pencil on white wove, 9⅞ x 12⅞″
l.r. "Boccioni"; u.r. and l.l. "I fidanzati"
T-36; W-x74

Verso: *Fragment of a Page with Arithmetical Figures, etc.*

Pencil
Unsigned

133. *Sheet with Three Studies of a Reclining Nude, and a Reclining Couple; Study for "The Dream: Paolo and Francesca."* 1908.

Pencil, pen and black ink with blue and ochre wash on white ruled paper, 6⅜ x 12⅛″
l.r. "Umberto Boccioni/908"
T-39; W-x87

134. *Agitated Crowd Surrounding a High Equestrian Monument.* 1908

Pencil, pen, brush and India ink on white wove, 14¼ x 9½″
u.r. "Umberto Boccioni/908"
T-55; W-x8

Verso: *Fragment of a City Plan*

Pencil
Unsigned

133

134

135. *Kneeling Allegorical Figure; Study for a Decorative Page Heading.* 1908

Pen, brush and black ink over pencil on tan wove with gray-blue threads, 9¼ x 7⅝″
l.r. "Boccioni"
T-56; W-204

136. *Allegorical Figure with Ledger; Study for a Decorative Page Heading.* 1908

Pen and black ink over pencil on white bristol board, 9⅜ x 11¾″
Unsigned
T-58; W-202

137. *Study for "Allegory of the Nativity."* 1908

Pencil, pen, brush and India ink on white wove, 9⅞ x 6⅝″
l.r. "UB"
T-61; W-x72

Verso: *Graffiti.*

Pen, brush and India ink
Unsigned

138. *Boccioni's Mother in Bed.* 1908

Pen and black ink on white wove, 7⅝ x 6″
l.r. "Umberto Boccioni"
T-47; W-172

139. *Boccioni's Sister in a Shawl Writing.* c. 1908-09

Pen and black ink on tan wove, 7½ x 5¾″
l.r. "Boccioni"
T-49; W-173

140. *Sheet of Studies with Bust of a Woman and Two Figure Compositions.* c. 1909

Pencil and India ink, 6½ x 7⅜″
l.c. "Boccioni"
T-51; W-x71

141. *Old Woman Eating.* c. 1908-09

Pen and ink on buff laid, 7 x 5⅞″
l.r. "Boccioni"
T-72; W-191

138

142

142. *Figure of an Old Woman.* c. 1909

Pencil on white wove, 7 x 2⅞″
l.r. "Boccioni"
T-79; W-x38

143. *Woman Leaning on a Chair (Boccioni's Sister).* c. 1909

Pencil on white wove, 15¾ x 14⅝″
l.c. "UB"
T-68; W-x15

144. *Study of a Woman in a Loose Robe.* c. 1909

Pencil on buff wove, 16¼ x 14⅞″
l.c. "UB"
T-69; W-127

145. *Head of a Horse with Blinkers,* c. 1909

Pen and India ink on white wove, 6⅛ x 4″
l.r. "Boccioni"
T-67; W-x52

146. *Landscape with Leafless Tree.* c. 1909

Pencil on buff wove, 5¾ x 7⅞″
l.r. "Boccioni"
T-124; W-x73 B

147. *Landscape with Geese.* c. 1909

Pencil and pen and black ink on buff laid, 5¾ x 10½″
l.r. "Boccioni"
T-125; W-167

148. *Street with Houses.* c. 1909

Crayon on white wove, 6⅝ x 4½″
l.r. "Boccioni"
T-189; W-x70

Verso: *Unidentifiable Fragment*

Crayon
l.r. "UB"

149. *Head of a Workman with Cap.* c. 1909

Pencil on buff wove, 6½ x 4¾″
l.l. "U. Boccioni"
T-80; W-206

Verso: *Summary Compositional Sketch*

Pencil
Unsigned

150. *Standing Workman with Cap.* c. 1909

Pencil on white wove, 7 x 3¾″
l.r. "UB"/"Boccioni"
T-81; W-x39

143

150

151

151   *Back of a Fashionably Dressed Woman.* c. 1909

Pencil on ivory wove, 6⅜ x 4⅛″
l.r. "Boccioni"
T-87; W-x65

Verso: *Man with a Brimmed Hat.*

Pencil
Unsigned

152.   *Workman from the Rear.* c. 1909-10

Pencil on white wove, 7⅛ x 4½″
l.l. "U. Boccioni"
T-82; W-x93

Verso: *Head of a Horse*

Pencil
Unsigned

153.   *Back of a Workman in Full Trousers.* c. 1909-10

Pencil on white wove, 6¾ x 3⅝″
l.l. "Boccioni"
T-84; W-x66

Verso: *Profile of a Standing Woman.*

Pencil
l.r. "UB"

154.   *Standing Workman with Arms Folded.* c. 1909-10

Pencil and crayon on white wove, 7 x 4½″
l.l. "UB"
T-85; W-x26

Verso: *Study of a Decanter and Stopper*

Pencil
Unsigned

155.   *Rear of a Walking Figure.* c. 1909-10

Pencil on white wove, 7⅛ x 4½″
l.r. "UB"; u.r. "Lolò"
T-86; W-179

156.   *Head and Nude Torso of a Workman.* c. 1909-10

Pencil on white wove, 6 x 4¼″
l.r. "U. Boccioni"
T-91; W-x37

Verso: *Fragment of a Sketch of a Reclining Woman*

Pencil
Unsigned

152

153

157. *Workman Wearing a Derby, Inverted Head of Man with Cap Lower Right.* c. 1910

Pencil on white wove, 6¾ x 3⅜″
l.l. "Boccioni"
T-90; W-x49

Verso: *Untitled*
Pencil
Unsigned

158. *Walking Man in a Rumpled Suit.* c. 1910

Pencil on white wove, 6½ x 4⅛″
l.r. "Boccioni"
T-93; W-178

159. *Study for "Giants and Pygmies"; Dramatic Composition of a Tree.* c. 1909-10

Pen and brownish-black ink on white wove, 6½ x 4⅛″
l.r. "Boccioni"
T-40; W-x21

160. *Reclining Male Nude.* c. 1909-10

Pencil on buff wove, 11⅞ x 7½″
l.l. "Umberto Boccioni"
T-95; W-139

Verso: *Graffiti and Study of a Foreshortened Hand*
Pencil
Unsigned

161. *Seated Male Nude.* c. 1909-10

Pencil on white wove, 15 x 10¼″
u.r. "UB"; l.r. "Boccioni"
T-97; W-138

Verso: *Seated Woman with Dark Blouse*
Pencil
l.r. "UB"

162. *Harnessed Horse with Feedbag.* c. 1909-10

Pencil on buff wove, 7 x 9⅛″
l.c. "UB"
T-104; W-x44

Verso: *Rear and Profile of Harnessed Horse*
Pencil
Unsigned

163. *Head of a Horse with Feedbag.* c. 1909-10

Pencil on white wove, 7⅛ x 4½″
l.r. "Boccioni"
T-105; W-x32

Verso: *Bust of a Man*
Pencil
Unsigned

157

162

164. *Head of a Woman.* c. 1909-10

Pencil on buff wove, 6⅝ x 4⅝"
l.r. "Boccioni"
T-127; W-143

Verso: *Head of a Woman*

Pencil
Unsigned

165. *Head of a Woman (Boccioni's Sister).* 1909-10

Pencil on white wove, 4⅞ x 4¾"
l.r. "Boccioni"
T-129; W-169

Verso: *Graffiti*

Pencil
Unsigned

166. *Young Woman Sewing.* 1909-10

Pencil on rough white wove, 9⅜ x 6¾"
l.r. "U. Boccioni"
T-128; W-171

167. *Seated Woman Reading.* 1909-10

Black, white and orange chalk on paper toned dark brown,
15¾ x 13⅞"
l.r. "Boccioni"
T-131; W-212

168. *Seated Woman Leaning on her Elbow.* 1909-10

Black, white and orange chalk and black ink on paper toned
dark gray, 15⅞ x 13½"
l.r. "Boccioni"
T-132; W-125

169. *Wheel Barrow.* 1909-10

Black, white and orange chalk on paper toned dark brown,
13½ x 11¾"
l.r. "Boccioni"
T-133; W-213

170. *Sheet of Studies with Two Portraits of a Man, related to
Bookplate, "In Letizia Ben Fare."* c. 1910

Pencil and pen and India ink on white wove, 6¾ x 4⅛"
l.r. "Boccioni"
T-44; W-x88

168

166

169

171. *Head of a Woman, possibly related to Bookplate,*
      "In Letizia Ben Fare." c. 1910

      Pencil on white wove, 6¾ x 4⅛″
      l.r. "Boccioni"
      T-45; W-x89

172. *Study of a Young Woman with Arms Raised, and of a*
      Female Face; related to Bookplate, "In Letizia Ben Fare."
      c. 1910

      Pencil on white wove, 6¼ x 4⅛″
      l.l. "Boccioni"
      T-46; W-144

      Verso: *Head of a Woman*

      Pencil
      Unsigned

173. *Sheet of Studies with Three Landscapes and Two Allegorical*
      Figures. c. 1910

      Pencil, pen and India ink on buff wove, 6½ x 6⅞″
      l.r. "Boccioni"
      T-65; W-x28

174. *Two Women Walking in Street Dress.* c. 1910

      Pencil on white wove, 6⅝ x 4⅝″
      l.r. "Boccioni"
      T-119; W-x9

      Verso: *Two Sketches of a Bust of a Workman, One Inverted.*

      Pencil
      Unsigned

175. *Two Standing Women in Street Dress.* c. 1910

      Pencil on white wove, 6½ x 4¼″
      l.r. "Boccioni"
      T-120; W-x16

      Verso: *Man in a Short Coat, and Study of a Paneled Door*

      Pencil
      l.r. "U Boccioni"

176. *Young Woman Reading (Ines).* 1910

      Charcoal over gray wash on rough white wove, 18⅜ x 13⅛″
      l.r. "U. Boccioni"
      T-136; W-123

177. *Self Portrait.* 1910

      Gray wash and pen with black ink on white wove,
      10¼ x 8¾″
      l.r. "21-I-910 / U. Boccioni"
      T-139; W-122

176

177

178. *Curly Haired Child (Fiammetta).* 1910

Pencil on white ruled paper, 12¾ x 8⅜″
l.r. "Boccioni"
T-142; W-x17

Verso: *Curly Haired Child (Fiammetta).* 1910

Pencil on white ruled paper
Unsigned
T-142 a; W-x107

179. *Curly Haired Child (Fiammetta).* 1910

Pencil on two joined sheets of ruled white paper,
16¾ x 12⅞″
l.r. "Boccioni"
T-143; W-x6

Verso: *Cursory Sketch of Figure (?).*

Pencil
Unsigned

180. *Curly Haired Child (Fiammetta).* 1910

Pencil on ruled white paper, 8¼ x 8¾″
Unsigned
T-144; W-x62

Verso: *Fragment*

Pencil
Unsigned

181. *Bust of a Woman with Black Hat.* c. 1910

Pencil on white wove, 7 x 4⅜″
l.r. "Boccioni"
T-146; W-x41

Verso: *Walking Horse with Feedbag*

Pencil
l.r. "UB"

182. *Study for "Modern Idol."* 1910

Pencil on white wove, 5¾ x 5¼″
l.r. "Boccioni"
T-148; W-x33

183. *Woman Reclining.* c. 1910

Pencil on tan wove, 9⅝ x 9″
l.r. "UB"
T-151; W-200

184. *Man Shoeing a Horse.* 1910

Pencil on white laid, 5¾ x 4¼″
l.r. "Boccioni"
T-152; W-x90

Verso: *Same Figure from the Front*

Pencil
Unsigned

180

182

185. *Study of the City with Overpass, Telephone Pole and Streetcar.* 1908-10

Pencil on ivory wove, 7¾ x 5½″
l.r. "Boccioni"
T-108; W-x73 C

186. *The Bridge of Gamboloita.* 1910

Charcoal, pen and ink on buff wove, 10⅞ x 9⅜″
l.r. "Boccioni/ponte di Gamboloita visto/dalla altalinea ferroviaria/ sufficientemente interessante/mattina 28 maggio 1910/abbastanza nuovo"
T-112; W-x60

187. *Crowd in Front of Corner Building.* 1910

Crayon on white wove, 7 x 9″
l.r. "U Boccioni"
T-154; W-x85
Nos. 187-193 are preliminary sketches for *The City Rises*

188. *Harnessed Horse.* 1910

Pencil on white laid, 4⅞ x 5⅞″
l.r. "Boccioni"
T-157; W-x43

Verso: *Muzzle and Neck of Horse*
Pencil
Unsigned

189. *Three Horses Tended by Men; Stone Pavement.* 1910

Pen and brush with India ink on white wove, 4½ x 6¼″
Unsigned
T-158; W-x97

Verso: *Horses and Figures in a Landscape.* 1910

Pen and India ink
l.r. "Boccini"
T-158 a; W-x103

190. *Man Leading a Horse.* 1910

Pencil on white wove, 4½ x 7″
l.r. "Boccioni"
T-159; W-x42

Verso: *Man*

Pencil and crayon
l.l. "UB"

191. *Composition Study for "The City Rises."* 1910

Pencil on white wove, 3⅞ x 6″
l.r. "UB"
T-161; W-40A

Verso: *Unidentifiable Subject*
Pencil
Unsigned

192. *Composition Study for "The City Rises."* 1910

Pencil on white wove, 5½ x 8¼″
l.r. "Boccioni"
T-162; W-x34

187

190

1

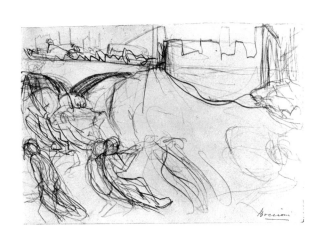

192

193. *Two Composition Sketches for "The City Rises" and Two for a Scene of an Urban Crowd.* 1910

Pencil on white wove, 5½ x 7⅛″
l.r. "Boccioni"
T-163; W-x40

Verso: *Group of Figures Related to Scene of Urban Crowd.* 1910

Pencil
Unsigned
T-163a; W-x102

194. *Composition Sketch for "Mourning."* 1910

Pen and ink on white wove, 6⅛ x 7⅜″
l.r. "Boccioni"
T-165; W-x84

195. *Study for "Mourning."* 1910

Pencil, charcoal, and blue and orange pencil with gray wash on buff wove, 9⅛ x 18½″
l.r. "Boccioni"
T-167; W-x54

196. *Sheet of Studies for "Mourning."* 1910

Pen and ink on double-ruled white wove, 6⅛ x 8¼″
l.r. "UB"
T-168; W-x98

197. *Study for "The Laugh."* 1910-11

Pencil on white wove, 4⅜ x 6″
l.r. "Boccioni"
T-173; W-x91

198. *Study for "The Laugh."* 1910-11

Pencil on white wove, 4½ x 5⅞″
l.r. "Boccioni"
T-174; W-x73 F

Verso: *Man with Moustache*

Pencil
Unsigned

199. *Study for "The Riot."* 1911

Pencil on white wove, 6⅛ x 6⅛″
l.r. "Boccioni"
T-178; W-x23

200. *Two Workmen; Study for "The Street Pavers."* 1911

Pencil on white wove partially discolored, 5⅜ x 8⅛″
l.r. "Boccioni"
T-179; W-61-58-320 A

193

195

196

197

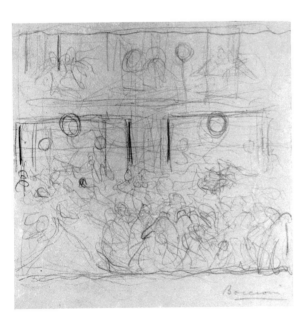

199

200

201. *Man Laying Paving Stones; Study for "The Street Pavers."*
1911

Pen and black ink on white wove, 5¾ x 8¼″
l.r. "Boccioni"
T-180; W-61-58-320B

202. *Portrait of a Young Man (Vico Baer?).* 1911

Pencil and gray wash on ivory wove, 11¾ x 9¾″
l.r. "1911"
T-181; W-209

203. *Boccioni's Sister Leaning on her Hand.* 1911

Pencil, pen and black ink on white wove, 8¼ x 6⅛″
l.r. "U. Boccioni"
T-182; W-170

204. *Planar Study of a Woman's Head (Ines?).* 1911

Pencil on white wove, 12¾ x 9¾″
l.r. "Boccioni"
T-183; W-135

Verso: *Profile of a Face*

Pencil
Unsigned

205. *Sketch for "Study of Women Amid Houses—Ines."* 1911

Pencil on white paper, 24 x 19⅛″
l.r. "1911 / U.B."
T-184; W-323

Verso: *Study for "States of Mind: The Farewells."* 1911

Pencil on white paper
l.r. "UB"
T-193; W-132

206. *Bald-Headed Man with Moustache.* c. 1911

Pencil on discolored white wove, 7⅛ x 5⅛″
l.r. "Boccioni"
T-185; W-207

207. *Analytical Study of a Woman's Profile.* 1911

Charcoal on buff wove, 4⅞ x 4⅞″
l.r. "Boccioni"
T-186; W-x19

208. *Analytical Study of Woman Seated on a Divan.* 1911-12

Pen and black ink on white paper, 8¼ x 12⅛″
Unsigned: l.r. "La seur [*sic*] de/par Boccioni" (by artist's hand)
T-187; W-x56

209. *Drawing after "States of Mind: Those Who Go."* 1912

Black ink over pencil on white wove, 12½ x 16¾″
Unsigned
T-201; W-DIA neg. 10949

210. *Head of Pietro Mascagni.* 1912

Pencil on white stationery bearing the letterhead of the Savoy Hotel, London, 8 x 10⅛″
l.l. "Boccioni"; l.r. "Mascagni"
T-203; W-153

Verso: *Caricatures of Pietro Mascagni and Queen Victoria.* 1912

Pencil
l.c. "Boccioni"; l.l. "La regina d'inghilterra"; u.r. "Londra marzo 1912/Mascagni futurista"; l.r. composer's autograph
T-203 a; W-322

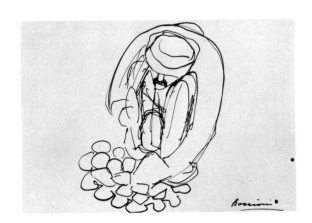

201

211. *Boccioni's Mother Sewing.* c. 1912

Pen and black ink on reddish-tan oiled paper, 9⅛ x 7¼″
Unsigned
T-204; W-184

Verso: *Standing Figure of a Woman*

Pen and brush and black ink
l.r. "Boccioni"

212. *Old Woman in Full Gown.* c. 1912

Pen and blue-black ink on white wove, 6 x 4¼″
l.r. "Boccioni"
T-205; W-192

213. *Boccioni's Mother Sewing.* c. 1912

Pen and black ink on reddish-tan oiled paper, 6¼ x 6⅛″
l.r. "Boccioni"
T-206; W-x95

Verso: *Sheet of Studies with Full-faced Head of Boccioni's Mother.* c. 1912

Pen and brush with black ink
Unsigned
T-206 a; W-x104

205. *(verso)*

207

209

214. *Analytical Study of a Woman's Head against Buildings.*
c. 1912

Pen and brownish-black ink on white wove, 11⅞ x 8½″
l.l. "Boccioni"
T-188; W-x11

215. *Bust of Boccioni's Mother.* 1912

Pencil on buff laid pasted on white paper, 8⅜ x 6⅝″
l.r. "Boccioni"
T-214; W-x48

216. *Bust of Boccioni's Mother; Study for "Abstract
Dimensions."* 1912

Pencil on buff laid pasted on white paper, 8⅜ x 6⅝″
l.r. "Boccioni"
T-215; W-x92

217. *Analytical Studies of the Head of Boccioni's Mother and
Another Female Head.* 1912

Pencil, pen and India ink on white laid, 6½ x 8⅝″
l.r. "Boccioni"
T-216; W-x18

218. *Analytical Study of Woman's Head against the Light with
Window Frame.* 1912

Pen and brownish ink on buff wove, 12⅞ x 8¼″
Unsigned
T-220; W-x27

219. *Head against the Light (Boccioni's Sister).* 1912

Pen and brown ink on buff wove, 5 x 4″
u.r. "Boccioni"
T-222; W-x68

220. *Study for the Sculpture "Fusion of a Head and a Window."*
1912

Pen and ink on white wove envelope, 5¾ x 4⅜″
l.r. "Boccioni"
T-224; W-x58

214

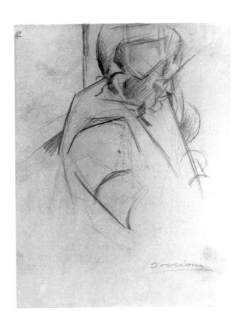

215

221. *Analytical Study of the Shoulder and Breast of a
Woman.* 1912

Pencil on white laid, 13 x 9½″
l.r. "Boccioni"
T-227; W-x13

222. *Group of Seated Men.* c. 1913
Pen on lined white wove, 7¾ x 5⅜″
Unsigned
T-207; W-164

223. *Man with Newspaper in a Café.* c. 1913
Pen and brownish ink on lined white wove, 8⅛ x 5⅜″
Unsigned
T-208; W-163

218

220

223

224. *Man at a Café Table, Paris.* c. 1913

Pen and brownish ink on lined white stationery from the Taverne de l'Hermitage, 8⅛ x 5⅜″
l.r. "Boccioni"
T-232; W-174

225. *Male Figure in Motion (Towards the Left).* 1913

Pencil on white wove, 6 x 4⅛″
T-234; W-x83

226. *Head of a Man; Study related to Collage "Dynamism of a Man's Head."* 1914

Pen and brownish-black ink on lined stationery from the Ristorante Savini, Milan, 8½ x 5¼″
l.r. "Boccioni"
T-279; W-175

227. *Caricature of Portly Man with Cigarette.* c. 1914

Brush and black ink on white laid, 12 x 8⅝″
l.r. "Boccioni"
T-280; W-208

228. *Head of Boccioni's Mother.* 1914-15

Pencil, pen and India ink, and blue-black wash on rough white wove, 12¼ x 9½″
l.r. "Boccioni"
T-278; W-x25

229. *Portrait of Silvia.* 1915

Pencil, gray wash, and black ink on heavy tan paper, 25⅜ x 18⅝″
u.r. "Boccioni"
T-293; W-131

230. *Portrait of Boccioni's Mother.* 1915-16

Black chalk, red, green and blue watercolor on buff wove, 25 x 20¼″
l.r. "Boccioni"
T-295; W-128

224

228

229

230

PRINTS

231. *Impression of Venice.* 1907

Etching printed in brownish black, 3¾ x 5⅝"
l.r. "U. Boccioni"
T-297; W-133

232. *Boccioni's Mother Crocheting.* 1907

Etching and drypoint printed in brownish black on
white wove, 14⅝ x 12⅛"
l.r. "U Boccioni"; on plate l.c. "1907" (printed in reverse)
T-299; W-x12

233. *Woman Resting on Sofa (Gisella).* 1907

Etching and drypoint in brownish black on cream
wove, 9⅝ x 13¼"
l.r. "U Boccioni"
T-306; W-x100

234. *Lovers and Swans in a Landscape.* c. 1908

Etching printed in colors, 8¼ x 12⅛"
l.r. "Boccioni"
T-302; W-158A

235. *The Kimono; Portrait of Ines.* c. 1909

Etching and drypoint printed in brownish black on
white wove, 7 x 5½"
l.r. "Umberto Boccioni"; on plate l.r. "Boccioni," on right
sleeve "INES"
T-303; W-160

236. *Sheet of Studies with Five Portraits.* c. 1909

Etching and drypoint printed in brownish black on
white wove, 7¼ x 11⅜"
l.r. "Umberto Boccioni"
T-304; W-x101 L

237. *Landscape with Industrial Plants.* 1909-10

Etching printed in brownish black on white wove, 3⅝ x 6"
l.r. "Umberto Boccioni"
T-307; W-x99

238. *Head of a Boy.* 1910

Etching printed in reddish brown on white wove, 5½ x 5⅛"
l.r. "U Boccioni" on plate l.l. "1910"
T-315; W-x53

239. *Woman and Child at the Table.* c. 1910

Etching printed in brown ink on white wove, 5⅝ x 9⅛"
l.r. "Umberto Boccioni"
T-310; W-211

240. *Boccioni's Mother Sewing.* c. 1910

Etching printed in brownish black on white
wove, 5½ x 4½"
l.r. "U Boccioni"
T-316; W-x22

232

Documents and Miscellany

GUILLAUME APOLLINAIRE

241. *L'Antitradition futuriste: manifeste = synthèse (The Futurist
Antitradition: manifesto = synthesis),* Paris, June 29, 1913
Pamphlet
11½ x 9⅛″

GIACOMO BALLA

242. *Il Vestito antineutrale: manifesto futurista (Anti-neutral
Clothing, Futurist Manifesto),* September 11, 1914
Pamphlet
11½ x 9⅛″

243. *Rose* (W-36)
Wood
13 x 9″

244. *Tree* (W-37)
Wood
13 x 10″

245. Palette and Two Brushes, c. 1925 (Made by the artist)
palette 8½ x 9″; brushes 9½ x 1″, 10½ x 1″

UMBERTO BOCCIONI

246. Palette
29⅝ x 17″

CONSTANTIN BRANCUSI

247. Two Sketches for the base of the *Blond Negress,* Paris,
1952 (G-757)
Pencil
8 x 3½″

ALEXANDER CALDER

248. Three Sketches for *Mobile,* 1949 (G-622)
Ink and pencil
10¾ x 8⅛″ each

MARCEL DUCHAMP

249. *Surrealism in 1947.* (W-130)
Book cover
10⁵⁄₁₆ x 9 x 3″

F. T. MARINETTI

250. *Manifeste du futurisme (Futurist Manifesto),* Le Figaro,
Paris, February 20, 1909
Pamphlet
11¼ x 18″

251. *L'Imagination sans fils et les mots en liberté: Manifeste
futuriste (Wireless Imagination and Words in Liberty:
Futurist Manifesto),* Milan, May 11, 1913
Pamphlet
11½ x 9⅛″

252. *La splendeur géométrique et méchanique et la sensibilité
numérique: manifeste futuriste (The Geometric and
Mechanical Splendor and the Numerical Sensibility:
Futurist Manifesto),* Milan, March 11, 1914
Pamphlet
11½ x 9½″

253. *Contre le luxe féminin: manifeste futuriste (Against Feminine
Luxury: Futurist Manifesto),* Milan, March 11, 1920
Pamphlet
11½ x 9⅛″

GINO SEVERINI

254. Documents pertaining to exhibition at Galleria Futurista,
Rome, 1913 (W-9)
Pencil and watercolor
2⅜ x 5½″; 7½ x 5¾″; 7¼ x 5½″

Documentation

Books

Taylor, Joshua C., "Harry Lewis Winston: Futurist and Other Twentieth-Century Art," *Great Private Collections,* ed. Douglas Cooper, introduction by Kenneth Clark, Macmillan, New York, 1963, pp. 292-303.

Baro, Gene, "Futurism Preserved: Lydia Winston Malbin," *The Collector in America,* compiled by Jean Lipman and the editors of *Art in America,* introduction by Alan Pryce-Jones, Viking Press, New York, 1971, pp. 180-189.

Articles

Saarinen, Aline B., "Collecting Modern Masters on a Master Plan," *Art News,* vol. 56, no. 6, October 1957, pp. 32-34, 64-66.

Degand, Leon and Jean Arp, "La Collection H[arry] et L[ydia] Winston au Musée de Détroit," *Aujourd'hui,* no. 15, December 1957, pp. 30-31.

"The Winston Collection on Tour," *Arts,* vol. 32, no. 4, January 1958, pp. 34-39.

Winston, Lydia Kahn and Harry, "Collecting Modern Art," *Vassar Alumnae Magazine,* vol. XLIII, no. 4, March 1958, pp. 10-13. Reprinted from *The Detroit Institute of Arts Catalogue,* 1957-58.

Edwards, Hugh, "Umberto Boccioni," *The Art Institute of Chicago Quarterly,* vol. LII, no. 2, April 1, 1958, pp. 25-28.

Mellquist, Jerome, "La Collection Winston," *XXe Siècle,* no. 11, Christmas 1958, n. p. Double issue.

Canaday, John, "True Story, Happy Ending—200 Drawings: Their Trip from Verona to Michigan," *The New York Times,* Sunday, July 23, 1961, p. 10.

Winston, Lydia Kahn, "Reflections on Art Collecting as a Creative Process," Wayne State University, November 29, 1961. On the occasion of a Special Convocation.

Winston, Lydia Kahn et Harry Lewis, "Le Futurisme," *Aujourd'hui,* no. 35, February 1962, pp. 4-13.

Francoeur, George, "The Winston Collection," *Chicago Mid-West Art,* vol. 3, no. 3, March 1967, pp. 7-9.

Baro, Gene, "Collector: Lydia Winston," *Art in America,* vol. 55, no. 5, September-October 1967, pp. 72-75.

Miesel, Victor H., "The 'heart' of The Winston Collection, Birmingham, Michigan," *The Connoisseur,* April 1968, pp. 259-263.

Exhibitions

Exhibitions which were composed partially of works from the Winston Collection are indicated by an asterisk. All other exhibitions listed were drawn entirely from the Winston Collection.

* The Detroit Institute of Arts, March 6-30, 1947, *A Loan Exhibition of French Paintings, XVII-XX Centuries.* Exhibition organized by Paul L. Grigaut.

Museum of Cranbrook Academy of Art, Bloomfield Hills, Michigan, November 8-25, 1951, *Mr. and Mrs. Harry Lewis Winston Collection.* Catalogue foreword by E.I.G.

The University of Michigan Museum of Art, Alumni Memorial Hall, Ann Arbor, Michigan, October 30-November 27, 1955, *20th Century Painting and Sculpture from The Collection of Mr. and Mrs. Harry Lewis Winston.* Catalogue text by Jean Paul Slusser.

Albion College, Albion, Michigan, April 10-25, 1956, *Selections from The Collection of Mr. and Mrs. Harry Lewis Winston, Birmingham, Michigan.* Exhibition organized by Vernon Bobbit; checklist.

The Detroit Institute of Arts, September 27-November 3, 1957, *Collecting Modern Art—Paintings, Sculpture and Drawings from The Collection of Mr. and Mrs. Harry Lewis Winston.* Exhibition organized by Paul L. Grigaut and Elizabeth Payne. Catalogue texts by Josef Albers, Jean Arp, Alexander Dorner, Benedetta Marinetti, Elizabeth Payne, Antoine Pevsner, E. P. Richardson, and Harry and Lydia Winston. Circulated by Institute of Contemporary Arts, Boston to Virginia Museum of Art, Richmond, December 13, 1957-January 5, 1958; San Francisco Museum of Art, January 23-March 13, 1958; Milwaukee Art Institute, April 11-May 12, 1958; Walker Art Center, Minneapolis, June 13-August 3, 1958.

The Art Institute of Chicago, March 14-April 27, 1958, *Boccioni: An Exhibition of Drawings and Prints from The Mr. and Mrs. Harry Lewis Winston Collection.* Exhibition organized by Hugh Edwards and catalogue essay by Marianne Martin.

Grand Rapids Art Museum, Michigan, December 3, 1959-January 2, 1960, *Exhibition of Greetings From Contemporary Artists from The Winston Collection.*

The Art Gallery of Windsor, Willistead Park, Windsor, Ontario, February 8-26, 1960, *Graphics and Drawings from The Winston Collection.* Exhibition organized by Kenneth Saltmarsh; checklist.

* The Detroit Institute of Arts, February 8-March 6, 1960, *Graphic Arts in Private Detroit Collections.* Exhibition organized by Paul L. Grigaut.

Palazzo Reale, Milan, April 30-June 26, 1960, *Arte italiana del XX secolo da collezione americane.* Travelled to Galleria Nazionale d'Arte Moderna, Rome, July 6-September 18, 1960. Exhibition organized by James Thrall Soby, International Council of The Museum of Modern Art, New

York. Special New York showing at Santini Brothers Warehouse, October 24 and 26, 1960.

Grand Rapids Art Museum, Michigan, March 1-April 7, 1961, *Graphics and Drawings from The Winston Collection;* checklist.

* The Museum of Modern Art, New York, May 31-September 5, 1961, *Futurism.* In coordination with The Detroit Institute of Arts, October 18-December 19, 1961 and Los Angeles County Museum of Art, January 14-February 19, 1962. Exhibition organized and catalogue introduction by Peter Selz. Catalogues *Futurism* and *The Graphic Work of Umberto Boccioni* by Joshua C. Taylor.

Flint Institute of Arts, Flint, Michigan, June 25-August 1, 1961, *Graphics and Drawings from The Winston Collection.* Exhibition organized by Dr. G. Stuart Hodge; checklist.

Stedelijk Museum, Amsterdam, April 19-May 28, 1962, *Umberto Boccioni—Drawings and Graphics by Umberto Boccioni from The Collection of Mr. and Mrs. Harry Lewis Winston.* The International Council of The Museum of Modern Art, New York. Exhibition organized by William S. Lieberman. Catalogue introduced by Willem Sandberg. Circulated by The Museum of Modern Art, New York, to J. B. Speed Art Museum, Louisville, Kentucky, November 2-23, 1962; University of Nevada Student Union, Reno, January 2-23, 1963; Washington University, St. Louis, Missouri, March 1-29, 1963; Miami Beach Art Center, Miami Beach, July 1-25, 1963; Reed College, Portland, Oregon, September 2-23, 1963; Arizona State University, Tempe, February 16-March 7, 1964; Western Washington State College, Bellingham, April 1-22, 1964; San Francisco State College, June 13-August 9, 1964.

* The Detroit Institute of Arts, January 10-February 4, 1962, *French Drawings and Watercolors from Michigan Collections.* Catalogue introduction by Paul L. Grigaut.

* The Detroit Institute of Arts, April 1-May 6, 1962, *American Paintings and Drawings from Michigan Collections.* Exhibition organized by Paul L. Grigaut.

* The Detroit Institute of Arts, May 1-June 6, 1962, *The Varied Works of Picasso.* Exhibition organized by Franklin Page.

J. B. Speed Art Museum, Louisville, Kentucky, November 7-December 30, 1962, *Greetings from The Lydia and Harry Winston Collection.* Exhibition organized by Franklin Page; checklist.

The University of Michigan Museum of Art, Alumni Memorial Hall, Ann Arbor, December 11, 1963-February 7, 1964, *Personal Greetings from Artists to Mr. and Mrs. Harry L. Winston;* checklist.

* The Detroit Institute of Arts, March 8-April 7, 1963, *The Dutch Contribution to The International Development of Art Since 1945.* Text written and original exhibition organized by Dr. Willem Sandberg; D.I.A. exhibition organized by Paul L. Grigaut.

J. B. Speed Art Museum, Louisville, Kentucky, January 7-February 2, 1964, *Leaders of Modern Art—Prints Lent by Mr. and Mrs. Harry L. Winston.* Exhibition organized by Franklin Page; checklist.

J. B. Speed Art Museum, Louisville, Kentucky, February 4-29, 1964, *Modern Prints—France (Lent by Mr. and Mrs. Harry L. Winston).* Exhibition organized by Franklin Page; checklist.

J. B. Speed Art Museum, Louisville, Kentucky, March 3-29, 1964, *Contemporary Prints—Low Countries (Lent by Mr. and Mrs. Harry L. Winston).* Exhibition organized by Franklin Page; checklist.

The Arts Council of Great Britain, London, September 19-October 17, 1964, *Umberto Boccioni: 1882-1916. An Arts Council exhibition of his graphic art from the collection of Mr. and Mrs. Harry Lewis Winston of Birmingham, Michigan.* Travelled to City Art Gallery, Manchester, October 31-November 21, 1964; City Art Gallery, Leeds, November 28-December 19, 1964; Art Gallery, Aberdeen, January 2-23, 1965. Catalogue foreword by Gabriel White and essay by Reyner Banham.

The Bloomfield Art Association, Birmingham, Michigan, March 13-23, 1966, *An Exhibition of Posters Designed by 20th Century Artists from The Collection of Mr. and Mrs. Harry L. Winston.* Exhibition organized by Arlen Linn.

Wayne State University, Detroit, April 12-May 2, 1966, *Posters By 20th Century Artists from The Winston Collection.*

Kresge Art Center Gallery, Michigan State University, East Lansing, October 2-30, 1966, *Posters by 20th Century Artists from The Lydia and Harry Lewis Winston Collection.* Exhibition organized by Paul Love.

The Bloomfield Art Association, Birmingham, Michigan, November 1-December 1, 1966, *Greetings from the Artists.* Exhibition organized by Arlen Linn.

Kresge Art Center Gallery, Michigan State University, East Lansing, March 5-26, 1967, *Winston Collection of Personal Greetings from 20th Century Artists.* Exhibition organized by Paul Love.

The Detroit Institute of Arts, April-May 1967, *Exhibition of Boccioni Drawings from The Lydia and Harry Lewis Winston Collection.* Exhibition organized by Ellen Sharp; checklist.

Ohio Wesleyan University, Delaware, Ohio, November 1-30. 1967, *Greetings from The Winston Collection.* Exhibition organized by Richard Wengenrath.

Henry Ford Community College, Dearborn, Michigan, December 1967-January 1968, *Posters from The Winston Collection.* Exhibition organized by George Francoeur.

First National Savings Bank, Detroit, January 3-March 4, 1968, *Posters of the 20th Century from The Lydia and Harry Lewis Winston Collection.*

Kresge Art Center, Michigan State University, East Lansing, Michigan, February 4-25, 1968, *Prints from The Winston Collection*. Statement by Lydia Winston Malbin, *Bulletin*, Kresge Art Center, vol. 1, no. 5, February 1968.

Gilmore Art Center, Kalamazoo Institute of Arts, Michigan, November 10-December 15, 1968, *Graphics from The Collection of Lydia and Harry Lewis Winston (Mrs. Barnett Malbin)*. Exhibition organized by Harry Greaver. Catalogue essay by Ellen Sharp.

The University of Michigan Museum of Art, Alumni Memorial Hall, Ann Arbor, February 16- March 16, 1969, *Graphics from The Collection of Lydia and Harry Lewis Winston*. Exhibition organized by Charles Sawyer; checklist and announcement.

The Detroit Institute of Arts, May 15-June 22, 1969, *Detroit Collects*. Exhibition organized by Samuel Wagstaff.

Krannert Art Museum, College of Fine and Applied Arts, University of Illinois, Champaign, October 12-November 16, 1969, *Extensions of the Artist: Prints from The Collection of Lydia and Harry Lewis Winston (Mrs. Barnett Malbin)*. Catalogue introduction by Muriel B. Christison; reprint of Wayne State University address by Lydia Winston Malbin.

The Bloomfield Art Association, Birmingham, Michigan, January 11-February 8, 1970, *Fifty Recent Graphics and Multiples Loaned by Dr. and Mrs. Barnett Malbin (The Lydia and Harry Lewis Winston Collection)*. Exhibition organized and catalogue introduction by Arlen Linn.

Kresge Art Center Gallery, Michigan State University, East Lansing, October 3-25, 1970, *Contemporary Prints from The Winston Collection*. Exhibition organized by Paul Love; checklist.

Indiana University Art Museum, Bloomington, February 10-March 21, 1971, *Reflection Thru a Collector's Eye: A selection of prints and drawings from the collection of Lydia and Harry Lewis Winston (Dr. and Mrs. Barnett Malbin)*. Exhibition organized by Thomas T. Solley and John Nozynski; catalogue essay by Ellen Sharp. Travelled to The University of Wisconsin, Milwaukee, March 30-April 30, 1971.

The Detroit Institute of Arts, February 15-March 15, 1971, *300 Posters from The Collection of Lydia Winston Malbin*. Exhibition organized by Samuel Wagstaff.

The UCLA Art Galleries, Los Angeles, September 19-October 31, 1971, *Posters from The Lydia and Harry Lewis Winston Collection/Mrs. Barnett Malbin, Birmingham, Michigan*. Exhibition organized by Frederick Wight; checklist.

University Art Gallery, Frick Fine Arts Building, University of Pittsburgh, December 14, 1971-January 16, 1972, *The Twentieth Century Print as Seen through The Lydia and Harry L. Winston Collection (Mrs. Barnett Malbin)*. Catalogue acknowledgements by Pamela Pierrepont Bardo and text by Robert Wang.

The Toledo Museum of Art, Ohio, April 2-30, 1972, *A Collector's Portfolio: An Exhibition of prints and posters from The Lydia and Harry Lewis Winston Collection (Dr. and Mrs. Barnett Malbin)*. Exhibition organized by Charles Gunther. Catalogue introduction by Otto Wittman and Norman Thal, Jr.

* The Detroit Institute of Arts, April 13-May 21, 1972, *Detroit Collects Prints and Drawings, Catalogue of an Exhibition of Prints and Drawings from Six Detroit Collections*. Exhibition organized and catalogue introduction by Ellen Sharp.

The University of Michigan Museum of Art, Alumni Memorial Hall, Ann Arbor, May 21-June 18, 1972, *Posters and Portfolios from The Collection of Lydia and Harry Lewis Winston*. Exhibition organized by Charles H. Sawyer; checklist.

The Detroit Institute of Arts, July 18, 1972- April 20, 1973, *Selections from The Lydia and Harry Lewis Winston Collection (Dr. and Mrs. Barnett Malbin)*. Checklist with introduction by Frederick J. Cummings.

The Society of The Four Arts, Palm Beach, Florida, February 3-March 4, 1973, *Collecting Prints and Sculpture . . . in all media*. Exhibition organized and catalogue introduction by John Gordon.

The Lydia and Harry Lewis Winston Collection

(Dr. and Mrs. Barnett Malbin)

A LISTING OF THE COLLECTION

Works included in the Guggenheim exhibition are marked by an asterisk. The listing is arranged alphabetically by artist and chronologically under each artist. The following is a list of abbreviations for various media: oil on canvas— o/c., gouache—g., watercolor—wc., collage—col., mixed media—m.m., etching—etch., lithograph—litho., serigraph—seri. Where not indicated, the support is paper.

Robert Adams	*Square Snake*	bronze	1956
Josef Albers	*Stripes in Blue*	oil on glass	1926
	* *Study for "Mirage A"*	oil on paper	1940
Pierre Alechinsky	*The Share of the Visible*	ink	1961
	Personages	ink	1961
Karel Appel	*Playthings*	g.	1949
	* *Head and Fish*	o/c.	1954
Alexander Archipenko	* *Nude No. 1*	crayon	c. 1912
	* *Nude No. 2*	crayon	c. 1912
Jean Arp	* *Head*	ink and pencil	c. 1920
	* *Abstract Form I*	ink	1922
	* *Abstract Form II*	ink	1922
	* *Bird Forms*	wood	1922
	Untitled	col.	c. 1922?
	* *Dream Column*	stone and bronze	1938; 1956
	* *Lunar Armor*	granite	1938
	Ganemede	bronze	c. 1950
	Composition	brass	c. 1954
Henry Bacon	*Portrait of Albert Kahn*	wc.	1891
	A Fountain	ink	1915
Jean Baier	*Untitled*	plastic (2)	1932
Giacomo Balla	* *Work*	o/c.	1902
	* *Spring Buds*	o/c.	c. 1906
	* *The Stairway of Farewells*	o/c.	c. 1908
	* *Study Related to "Abstract Velocity"*	g.	c. 1913
	* *Study for "Mercury Passing before the Sun."*	g.	1914
	* *Goldfish*	pastel	c. 1914
	* *Vortex + Line of Velocity*	pencil	c. 1914-15
	* *Futurist Necktie*	wc., g. and pencil	c. 1916
	* *The Injection of Futurism*	o/c.	c. 1918
	* *Path of a Gunshot*	o/c.	c. 1918
	* *Self Portrait*	ink	c. 1920
	* *Iridescent Interpenetration*	o/c.	
	* *Fist of Boccioni*	cardboard, wood and paint	
	* *Crowd and Landscape*	col.	
	* *Rose*	painted wood	
	* *Tree*	painted wood	
Gerrit Benner	*Composition*	o/c.	1961
	Flowers	pencil	1963
Maria Blanchard	* *Composition with Figure*	o/c.	1916
Umberto Boccioni	* *Self Portrait*	o/c.	c. 1908
	* *The Street Pavers*	o/c.	1911
	* *Anti-Graceful; The Mother*	bronze	1912
	* *Development of a Bottle in Space*	bronze	1912-13
	* *Unique Forms of Continuity in Space*	bronze	1913
	* *Study for "The Drinker"*	oil, g. and col.	1914

A complete listing of the Boccioni drawings and prints in the Winston/ Malbin Collection is found in Joshua C. Taylor's *The Graphic Work of Umberto Boccioni*, The Museum of Modern Art, New York, 1961. The drawings total 179 sheets with 82 versos, making a total of 261 actual drawings.

Georges Braque	* Cards and Dice	o/c.	c. 1914
Constantin Brancusi	* The Blond Negress	bronze	1933
	* Sketch for Base of		
	The Blond Negress	pencil	1952
	Pyramid of the Fatal	pencil	1952
Erich Buchholz	The Beginning of The Cross	gesso on wood	1922
Alberto Burri	Grand Ferro M-6	col., sheet metal	1958
Alexander Calder	Final Sketch for Winston		
	Mobile	ink and pencil	1949
	Three Sketches for Mobile	ink	1949
	* Three Sketches for Winston		
	Mobile	ink and pencil	1949
	* Mobile	painted metal	1949
Carlo Carrà	* The Night of January 20, 1915,		
	I Dreamed This Picture		
	(Joffre's Angle of Penetration		
	on the Marne against		
	Two German Cubes)	col.	1914-15
Christoa Capralos	The Poet and his Muse	bronze	1960
	Zeus and Hera	bronze	1961
César	Iron Bird	iron	1957
Marc Chagall	Dream—Young Child and		
	Fortune	g.	1929
Edouardo Chillida	Composition	col. and ink	1953
Pietro Consagra	Colloquies	bronze	n.d.
William Copley	Nude on Divan	ink	1964
	Composition with Figure	ink	1965
Corneille	Springtime Panoply	o/c.	1962
(Cornelius van Beverloo)			
Wessel Couzijn	Icarus	bronze	n.d.
	Broken Light	crayon	1962
Hubert Dalwood	Object; Open Space	aluminum	1959
	King	aluminum	1960
Alan Davie	Trick for the King	oil on board	1960
Edgar Degas	Dancer Tying her Slipper	pastel	n.d.
Eugène Delacroix	Male Classical Figure	wc. and sepia	n.d.
	Figures Two Sketches:		
	Bust, and Right Shoulder		
	of Woman	pencil	n.d.
Robert Delaunay	* Still Life With Red		
	Tablecloth	o/c.	1937
Narcisse Virgile de la	Flower Picture	o/c.	n.d.
Pena Diaz			
Theo van Doesburg	* Still Life	o/c.	1916
Piero Dorazio	Ubiquita	painted wood	1955
	Untitled	ink and wash	1958
	Romance	o/c.	1959
	Abstract	bronze	n.d.

Joseph D. Downing	*Untitled*	col.	1966
	Staplage No. 1	col.	c. 1964
	Staplage No. 2	col.	c. 1964
	Staplage No. 3	col.	c. 1966
	Untitled	wc.	c. 1971
Jean Dubuffet	*Figure*	o/c.	1954
	The Joker	clinker	1954
Marcel Duchamp	*Valise Containing Miniature Reproductions of the Work of the Artist*	m.m.	1941-42 and 1952
	Set of Discs and Record Attachment to Go on a Turntable, such as a Record Player or any Fixture to Create Movement	m.m.	1961
Max Ernst	* *Sitting Buddha*	col. and print	1920
	* *Composition*	o/c.	1924-26
	* *Come into the Continents*	pencil, crayon	1926
Paul Feeley	* *Katadoro*	plastic paint on canvas	1963
	Dabih	wood	1965
Lyonel Feininger	*Fishing Smacks*	wc.	1942
	Boats	wc.	1943
Lucio Fontana	*Study for the Doors of the Milan Cathedral*	ceramic	n.d.
David Fredenthal	*Head of a Girl Looking at Hands*	pencil	c. 1940
Otto Freundlich	* *The Unity of Life and Death*	o/c.	1936-38
Naum Gabo	*Linear Construction in Space No. 1*	plastic and nylon thread	c. 1950
Alberto Giacometti	* *The Couple*	bronze	1926
Emile Gilioli	*Chimera*	onyx	1956
Albert Gliezes	* *The Bather*	o/c.	1912
Julio Gonzalez	* *Woman with Broom*	iron	1929-30
	* *The Kiss*	iron	1930
Juan Gris	* *Man with Guitar*	pencil	1918
	* *The Siphon Bottle*	o/c.	1919
Pegeen Guggenheim	*Tea Party*	o/c.	1945
Etienne Hajdu	*The Bud*	ceramic	1949
	The Siren	marble	1956
Jean Hélion	*Yellow Stripes*	o/c.	1938
Auguste Herbin	* *Composition*	o/c.	1921
Rudolf Hoflehner	*Goddess of the Mediterranean*	iron	1958
Johan B. Jongkind	*St. Pierre or View of a Village*	wash and pencil	1861
	Moonlight	o/c.	1872

Asger Jorn	*The Suicide of Mr. H.*	o/c.	1961
Albert Kahn	*European Sketch*	wc.	c. 1890
	Sketch of Chateau		
	Blois, France	wc.	c. 1890
	Wrotham	pencil	1925
	Taxco	pencil	1937
	St. Germain des Près	pencil	n.d.
Vasily Kandinsky	* *Luminosity*	o/c.	1927
	* *De Profundis*	wc.	1932
	Light Cubes	wc.	1932
Angelica Kauffman	*Diana and the Nymphs*	wc.	n.d.
Paul Klee	*Munich*	ink	1910
	* *What Remains*	g. and charcoal	c. 1926
	* *Forged Still Life*	wc.	1937
	* *Signs in Blue*	wc. on tinted cloth	c. 1938
Kotchar	*Figure*	paint on iron	1932
Aris Koutroulis	*Untitled*	pastel	1969
Frans Krajcberg	*Composition*	g.	1959
	Composition	g.	1960
Yasuo Kuniyoshi	*Head of a Young Girl*	oil	1937
Gaston Lachaise	* *Woman—Arms Akimbo*	bronze	c. 1910-12
	* *Woman Arranging Hair*	bronze	c. 1910-12
Roger de La Fresnaye	* *Study for "The 14th of July"*	wc.	1913
	* *Composition with a Trumpet*	ink and wash	1918
Louis Latapie	*Dream Caryatid*	o/c.	1953
Henri Laurens	* *Man with a Moustache*	stone	1919?
Caroline Lee	*The Buoy*	aluminum	1971
Fernand Léger	* *Woman in Armchair*	o/c.	c. 1912-13
	* *Still Life*	pencil	1921
Les Levine	*Windows*	col.	1969
	Windows	col.	1969
Mon Levinson	*Overlapping Squares in Flux*	plexiglas, paper and ink	1967
	Untitled	pencil	1972
El Lissitzky	* *Proun No. 95*	col., g., oil	c. 1920-23
Morris Louis	* *Quo Numine Lasso*	m.m.	1959
	* *Late Flowering*	acrylic resin on unsized duck	1962
Lucebert (L. C. Swanswijk)	*Family Portrait*	g.	1960
Stanton MacDonald-Wright	* *Conception Synchromy*	o/c.	1916-17?
Alberto Magnelli	*Untitled*	col.	1949
André Masson	* *Nude under Fig Tree*	charcoal and ink	1944
Louis Marcoussis	*Loreley*	o/c.	1932
John Marin	*Small Pointe, Maine*	wc.	1914
	Near Stonington, Maine	wc.	1915
Henri Matisse	* *The Velvet Gown*	ink	1936
Bernard Meadows	*Shot Bird*	bronze	1958
	Shot Bird	bronze	1959

Jean Metzinger	* Still Life with Pears	o/c	1912-17
	Still Life with Pipe	o/c	1916
Pierre Mignot	No. VIII	ink	1969
	No. X	ink	1969
Mirko	Woman Drinking at a River	bronze	c. 1954
Joan Miró	* Personage; Fratellini	o/c	1927
	Figures and Bird in		
	Front of the Sun	o/c	1930
Piet Mondrian	* Composition in Black and		
	White with Blue Square	o/c	1935
Claude Monet	Water Lilies or Nymphiades	o/c	1907
Richard Mortensen	Cahier de Marseilleiu	g.	1959
Adolph J.T. Monticelli	In The Park or Garden		
	Scene with Seven Ladies	o/c	n.d.
Henry Moore	* Abstract Sculpture	hoptonwood stone	1937
Louise Nevelson	Personage One plus Two	terra cotta	c. 1947
Gordon Newton	Untitled No. 1	charcoal	n.d.
	Untitled No. 2	charcoal	n.d.
Kenneth Noland	* Baba Yagga	acrylic resin on unsized canvas	1964
David Packard	Balled Head	bronze	1962
Eduardo Paolozzi	* Head	bronze	1957
Chong Bae Park	Untitled	cast iron	1967
Antoine Pevsner	* Square Relief	plastic on cardboard	1922
	* Figure	copper	1925
	* Fresco, Fauna of the Ocean	brass and tin	1944
Francis Picabia	* Landscape, La Creuse	o/c.	c. 1912
	* Mechanical Expression		
	Seen through Our Own		
	Mechanical Expression	wc.	1913
	* Portrait of Marie Laurencin	wc.	c. 1917
	* Alarm Clock I	ink	1919
Pablo Picasso	* Still Life	pencil	1913
	* Glass on a Table	col.	1914
	* Still Life with Guitar (recto);		
	The Portal (Fontainbleu)		
	(verso)	o/c.	1921
	* Portrait of a Woman		
	Seated under a Light	ink and wash	1938
	* Portrait of Dora Maar	o/c.	1941
Jackson Pollock	* Moon Vessel	o/c.	1945
Enrico Prampolini	Mechanical Venus	col. and oil on wood	1930
	Polimaterico Automatismo A	col.	1940
	Polimaterico Automatismo C	col.	1940
	Polimaterico Automatismo F	col. and oil on board	1941

Germaine Richier	*Praying Mantis*	bronze	1947
	The Six-Headed Horse	gilded bronze	1953-56
Medardo Rosso	* *The Flesh of Others*	wax over plaster	1883
	* *Sick Boy*	wax over plaster	1883
	* *Man in Hospital*	bronze	1889
	* *Jewish Boy*	wax over plaster	1892
	* *Ecce Puer*	wax over plaster	1906-07
Morgan Russell	* *Synchromy No. 2*		
	To Light	o/c. mounted on cardboard	1913?
Luigi Russolo	* *Perfume*	o/c.	c. 1908
Emilio Scanavino	*Reliquie*	oil	1959
Kurt Schwitters	* *Composition: Ashoff, Ellen*	col.	1922
	* *C.48 S.Y. Cut-Merz*	col.	1946
	* *S.55 Merz*	col.	1946
	* *Ent Garett, Merz*	col.	1947
	* *Examiner 2861 Merz*	col.	1947
Michel Seuphor	*Untitled*	ink	n.d.
	Velvet Dance	col. and g.	1958
Gino Severini	* *Study for "Portrait of Mme. M.S."*	pastel	1912
	* *Three Documents Pertaining to Futurist Exhibition*	wc.	1913
	* *Portrait of Mme. Severini*	wc.	1913
	* *Still Life with Cherries*	col., pencil and crayon	1913
	* *Study for "Sea = Dancer"*	charcoal	1913
	* *Sea = Dancer; Dancer beside The Sea*	o/c. with sequins	1913-14
	* *Study for Armored Train*	pencil	1914
	Drawing	ink	1951
	Abstraction	ink and pastel	1952
	Abstraction	g.	1952
	Untitled	ink	1958
	Untitled	wc. and ink	1963
	Still Life with Epinette	mosaic	n.d.
Mario Sironi	* *Composition*	g.	1912
	The Dancer	g.	1913
	* *Man on Motorcycle*	col. and oil	1918
Tony Smith	*Piece*	wood	1966-68
	Rhomboidal Dodecahedron	wood	1970
	Spitball	granite	1971
Francesco Somaini	*Wound—Great Wounded One No. 1*	lead	1960
Chaim Soutine	*The Red Gladiolas*	o/c.	c. 1919
Nicholas de Stael	*Abstraction*	wc.	1950
Frank Stella	* *Sketch Red Lead*	o/c.	1964
Peter Stroud	*Green Circumvent with Blue*	politec on masonite	1964
Yves Tanguy	* *Shadow Country*	o/c.	1927
Mark Tobey	* *Battle of the Lights*	g.	1956

Joaquín Torres-García	Composition	painted wood	c. 1931
	* Symmetrical Composition	o/c.	1931
Tristan Tzara	Fragment signed by Tristan Tzara, Léon Degand and others	ink	1956
Laurence Vail	Figure No. 1	tin, glass and found objects	n.d.
	Figure No. 2	tin, glass and found objects	n.d.
Victor Vasarely	Ixion	oil on glass	c. 1964
Andy Warhol	* Self Portrait	m.m.	1967
Tom Wesselmann	Study for Still Life	pencil	1963
Richard Wilt	Du Geant Poryphyrion	acrylic/c.	1969

II INDIVIDUAL GRAPHICS (partial listing)

Henri-Georges Adam	Snares	litho.	1959
Anni Albers	Triadic Series C, D, E, F	seri.	1969
Josef Albers	Seclusion	litho.	1942
	Solo V	intaglio	1958
Karel Appel	Composition	litho.	1958
	Composition	litho.	1959
	Flying Birds	litho.	1959
Alexander Archipenko	Still Life	litho.	n.d.
Jean Arp	Everday Magic	woodcut	1961
	Untitled	etch.	n.d.
Sophie Taeuber-Arp	Abstraction	litho.	n.d.
Olle Baertling	from Album "The Angles of Baertling"	seri. (3)	1965-68
Willi Baumeister	Summetic Landscape	litho	n.d.
Roger Bissière	Rose	etch.	n.d.
Robert Broner	Migrations	litho.	1958
Alexander Calder	Quilt	litho.	1966
	Flying Saucers	litho.	1968
Mary Callery	A Study for Sculpture	litho.	n.d.
Massimo Campigli	The Theater	litho.	1951
Patrick Caulfield	Glasses and Bottle	seri.	n.d.
César	Composition	litho.	n.d.
	Untitled	litho.	1970
Marc Chagall	Romantic Figure	etch. and wc.	n.d.
Teng Beng Chew	State I: Conglomeration	litho.	1967
Christo (Javacheff)	Corridor Store Front	m.m.	1967
Corneille	Summer Games	litho.	1960
	Southern Sea	litho.	1961
Wessel Couzijn	Moving Forms	etch.	n.d.
	Composition No. 1, No. 2, No. 3	litho.	1963

Allan D'Arcangelo	Landscape	silkscreen	1968
Alan Davie	Zurich Improvisations, No. 17	litho.	n.d.
Maurice Estève	Aladdin	litho.	n.d.
Helen Frankenthaler	Sky-Frame IV	monotype	1964
	What Red Lines Can Do	seri.	1970
Antonio Frasconi	The Dog and the Crocodile	woodcut	1952
Rupprecht Geiger	Untitled	seri.	1968
Marcel Gromaire	Reclining Woman	etch.	1950
Hans Hartung	Abstraction	litho.	n.d.
	L6	litho.	1966
Stanley William Hayter	Abstraction	intaglio	n.d.
Al Held	Untitled I	seri.	1966-68
Anton Heyboer	Untitled	etch.	1962
Sue Carol Hirtzel	Black Set 2	intaglio	1972
Howard Hodgkin	Girl on a Sofa	litho.	1968
Robert Indiana	Love	seri.	n.d.
Jasper Johns	Hatteras	litho.	1963
Allen Jones	Slipper	litho.	1968
Asger Jorn	from Jubilaeum-serien	litho.	1963
Vasily Kandinsky	Kleine Welten I; III	litho.	1922
	Kleine Welten VII; VIII	woodcut	1922
	Kleine Welten IX; X; XI	etch.	1922
Ellsworth Kelly	Cyclamen III	litho.	1964
	No. 4 Vert	litho.	n.d.
Aris Koutroulis	Veil No. 1; No. 2	cliche verre	1968
Yasuo Kuniyoshi	Acrobat	litho.	n.d.
	Still Life at the Window	litho.	1928
Marie Laurencin	Two Girls and a Dog	litho.	n.d.
Henri Laurens	Horizontal Figure	litho.	c. 1935
	Nude Female Figure	litho.	c. 1935
Julio le Parc	Untitled	litho.	n.d.
	Untitled	litho.	n.d.
Les Levine	Disposables	plastic multiple (3 clear)	1969
Alexander Liberman	Untitled	litho.	1970
Roy Lichtenstein	Head of a Girl	litho.	n.d.
	Stedelijk	litho.	n.d.
Vincent Longo	Swinging White	woodcut	1958
	Keeping Still	etch.	1964
	Screen	etch.	1967
	Green Screen	etch.	1967
	Other Side	etch.	1967
	Plaid	aquatint and etch.	1968
	Frontal	etch.	1970
Lucebert	Klein Circus	etch.	n.d.
	Geheime Raad	etch.	1961

Alfred Manessier	*Abstraction*	litho.	n.d.
Marino Marini	*Man and Two Horses*	litho.	c. 1951
Paul Martyka	*171 Cubes*	intaglio	1972
André Masson	*Mythology of Being*	etch.	1942
	Nocturnal Notebook	etch.	1944
Henri Matisse	*Mother and Child*	litho.	c. 1951
Joan Miró	*Lithograph IV*	litho.	1944
	Untitled	etch.	1947
	Untitled	etch.	1947
	Cartones	litho.	1959-65
Amedeo Modigliani	*Reclining Nude*	etch.	n.d.
Rolf Nesch	*The Blue Mask*	intaglio	1959
Louise Nevelson	*The Great Wall*	intaglio	1970
Barnett Newman	*The Moment*	seri. on plexiglas	1966
Claes Oldenburg	*New Media, New Forms*	litho.	n.d.
	Soft Scissors	litho.	1968
Pablo Picasso	*Owl Head*	litho.	n.d.
	Untitled	litho.	n.d.
	Don Quixote	litho.	1955
Serge Poliakoff	*Composition*	etch.	1958
Robert Rauschenberg	*Stunt Man I; II; III*	litho.	1962
	Accident	litho.	1963
	Front Roll	litho.	1964
Man Ray	*Untitled*	etch.	n.d.
Germaine Richier	*Praying Mantis*	etch.	c. 1947
Bridget Riley	*Fragment*	seri. on plexiglas	1965
Larry Rivers	*Ford Chassis I*	litho.	1961
Sally W. Robinson	*Rhythms*	litho.	1969
	Purple Grid	litho.	1972
	Floral Garden	cliche verre	1973
Georges Rouault	*Clown Tristis*	aquatint	1934
	Busts of Two Women	litho.	n.d.
Luigi Russolo	* *Neitzsche*	etch.	c. 1909
Michel Seuphor	*August*	seri.	1964
	Game in the summer '71	seri.	1971
Richard Smith	*Edward Gordon Craig Series II*	litho.	1968
Pierre Soulages	*Composition*	litho.	n.d.
Andrew Stasik	*Untitled*	litho.	1958
René Pierre Tal Coat	*Composition*	litho.	1958
Yves Tanguy	*Surrealist Figure*	etch.	n.d.
Jean Tinguely	*Untitled*	litho.	c. 1969
Mark Tobey	*Untitled*	etch.	1967

Henri Toulouse-Lautrec	*Marcelle Lender Doing the Bolero in the Operetta "Chilperie"*	litho.	n.d.
	Au Moulin Rouge, L'Union Franco-Russe	litho.	n.d.
Maurice Utrillo	*Montmartre*	litho.	n.d.
	Montmartre Le Moulin de la Galette	litho.	n.d.
	Notre Dame	litho.	n.d.
	Paris Street Scene	litho.	n.d.
Victor Vasarely	*Untitled*	seri.	1963
Jacques Villon	*Figures at a Table*	litho.	n.d.
	Figures	etch.	1951
June Wayne	*Goe and Catche a Falling Starre*	litho.	1957

III PORTFOLIOS OF GRAPHICS (partial listing)

Anni Albers	*Triadic Series*	screenprints (4)	1969
Josef Albers	*Homage to the Square Soft Edge-Hard Edge*	litho.	1965
	Ten Variants	litho.	1967
Accardi, Colla, Dorazio, Festa, Fontana, Iosavio, Rotella, Sanfilippo, Schifano and Scialoja	*La Litografia: Galleria La Salita Robra*	litho. (1 by each artist)	1963
Jean Arp	*L, Rue Gabrielle*	etch. (12)	1958
Afro, Balla, Conte, Dorazio, Jarema, Magnelli, Moretta, Munari, Nativi, Perilli, Prampolini, Radice, Severini, Soldati	*Arte Astratta Italia*	seri. (1 by each artist)	1955
Giuseppe Capogrossi	*Untitled*	litho. (6)	n.d.
Genevieve Claisse	*Cercles*	seri. (12)	1967
Arp, Sonia Delaunay, Magnelli, and Taeuber-Arp	*Aux Nourritures terrestres*	litho. (10)	1950
Sonia Delaunay	*Compositions couleurs idées*	litho. (40)	n.d.

Max Ernst	*Les Chiens ont soif*	etch. (2); litho. (25)	1964
	Histoire Naturelle, signed	collotypes after original frottages (34)	1926
Gottfried Honegger	*Transmissions*	litho. (5)	1954
Warja de Honegger-Lavater	*Chacun sa chimère*	etch. (5)	1953
Les Levine	*Iris, Print-out Portrait*	litho. (9)	1969
André Masson	*Mythology of Being: A Poem*	etch. (9)	1942
Carlos Merida	*Estampas del popol vuh*	litho. (10)	1943
Joan Miró	*Untitled*	litho. (13)	1948
Richard Mortensen and Victor Vasarely	*A l'Occasion de l'exposition "Mortensen/Vasarely"*	seri. (6)	1967
Ad Reinhardt	*Untitled*	seri.	1966
Michel Seuphor	*Intimes étendures*	seri. (10)	1961
Andrew Stasik	*Prints and Poems*	intaglio (9)	1958
Georges Valmier	*Collection décors et couleurs*	color reproduction (20)	n.d.
Stuart Davis, Indiana, Kelly, Lichtenstein, Motherwell, Ortman, Poons, Reinhardt, Stella, Warhol	*Ten Works by Ten Painters*	seri.	1964

IV POSTERS: DESIGNED BY THE ARTISTS (partial listing)

Jean Arp	Galerie Denise René, Paris	litho.	1960
	Staatliche-Kunsthalle, Baden-Baden	litho.	1960
	Moderna Museet, Stockholm	litho.	1962
	Galerie Denise René, Paris	litho.	1962-63
	Del Vetro D'Azie, Venice	litho.	1964
	Louis Broder Editeur, Paris	litho.	1966
	Galerie Im Erker am Gallusplatz, St. Gallen	litho. (3)	1967
	Museo D'Arte Contemporanea Locarno	photomontage	n.d.

Alexander Calder	Galerie Maeght, Paris, signed	litho.	n.d.
	Galerie Maeght, Paris, signed	litho.	n.d.
	Galleria Dell'Obelisco, Rome	litho.	1956
	Fondation Maeght, St. Paul	litho.	1969
Marcel Duchamp	Sidney Janis Gallery, New York	litho.	1953
	Musée National D'Art Moderne, Paris	litho.	1967
	The Bride Stripped Bare . . .	m.m.	n.d.
Fernand Léger	Maison de la Pensée Française, Paris	litho.	1951
	Maison de la Pensée Française, Paris, signed	litho.	1954
	Grand Palais, Paris	litho.	1971
Jean Lurçat	Maison de la Pensée Française, Paris, signed	litho.	1952
Henri Matisse	Maison de la Pensée Française, Paris	litho.	1950
	Grand Palais, Paris	litho.	1970
Joan Miró	Galerie Maeght, Paris	litho. (5)	n.d.
	Galerie Maeght, Paris	litho.	1971
Pablo Picasso	Maison de la Pensée Française, Paris, signed	litho.	1948-49
	Musée des Arts Décoratifs Pavillon de Marsan, Paris	litho.	1955
	Vallauris, signed	litho.	1956
	Vallauris, signed	litho.	1956
	* Galeries 65 Cannes	litho.	1956
	Galerie Beyeler, Basel, signed	litho.	1956
	Galerie Lucie Weill, Paris	litho. & col.	1956
	Galerie Beyeler, Basel signed	litho.	1957
	Vallauris, signed	woodblock	1957
	Exposition de Céramiques, signed	litho.	1958
	Maison de la Pensée Française, Paris, signed	litho.	1958
	Affiches orignales des maitres de l'Ecole de Paris	litho.	1959
	* Galerie de Remparts, Antibes	litho. (2)	1959
	Los Angeles County Museum of Art	litho.	1959
	Galerie Beyeler, Basel	litho.	1967
	Galerie Beyeler, Basel, signed	litho.	1970
	Musée National d'Art Moderne, Paris	litho.	1971
	Galerie de Passeur, Paris	litho. (2)	1971

Robert Rauschenberg	Dwan Gallery, New York	litho.	n.d.
	Jewish Museum, New York, signed	litho.	1963
	St. Louis Symphony Hall, signed	litho.	1968
Willem Sandberg	Israel Museum, Jerusalem, signed	litho.	1968
Gino Severini	Galerie Berggruen, Paris, signed	litho.	1966
Ben Shahn	Musée National d'Art Moderne, Paris, signed	litho.	1954
Andy Warhol	Ferus Gallery, Los Angeles	litho.	n.d.
	Morris International, Toronto	litho.	1965
	Galerie Thomas, Dusseldorf	seri.	1970
Tom Wesselman	Galerie Thomas, Dusseldorf	litho.	1968

V RARE BOOKS containing original graphics (partial listing)

Josef Albers	*Interaction of Color,* Yale University Press, 1963
Karel Appel	Hugo Claus, *Karel Appel, Painter,* Abrams, 1952
Jean Arp	*Dreams and Projects,* Fequet & A. Baudia, 1951-52
Georges Braque	Tristan Tzara, *La Bonne Heure,* R. Jacquet, 1955
Cobra	Monographs of works of artists in the Cobra Group, 1950
Constant	Gerrit Konwenaar, *Goede Morgan Haan,* Experimentale Groep, 1949
Marcel Duchamp	*Le Surréalisme en 1947,* Maeght, 1947
Futurism	ed. Vanni Scheiwiller, *Piccola antologia di poeti futuristi,* Milan, 1958
Albert Gleizes and Jean Metzinger	*Du Cubisme,* Compagnie Française des Arts Graphiques, 1947
Henri Laurens	Homer, *L'Odyssée,* Creuzevault, 1952
Fernand Léger	Tristan Tzara, *La Face intérieure,* Seghers, 1953
Louis Marcoussis	*Planches de salut,* Jeanne Bucher, 1931
André Masson	*Nocturnal Notebook,* Curt Valentin, 1944
	Georges Duthuit, *Le Serpent dans la galere,* Curt Valentin, 1945
Joan Miró	Tristan Tzara, *Parler seul poeme,* Maeght, 1948, 1950
	Miró-Cartones, 1959-1965, Pierre Matisse Gallery, 1965
Mehmed D. Nejad	Tristan Tzara, *Le Temps naissant,* 1955
Antoine Pevsner	Carola Giedion-Welcker, *Antoine Pevsner,* Neuchâtel, 1961
Pablo Picasso	Tristan Tzara, *A Haute flamme,* Jacquet, 1955
Pierre-Auguste Renoir	Ambroise Vollard, *La Vie et l'oeuvre de Pierre-Auguste Renoir,* Vollard, 1919
Willem Sandberg	*Nu-XX,* Holland, 1959
Joaquín Torres-García	*La Ciudad sin nombre,* Montevideo, 1941
Jacques Villon	Tristan Tzara, *Miennes,* Caractères, Paris, 1955

VI ARTISTS AS ILLUSTRATORS (partial listing)

Pierre Bonnard	*Parallèlement*	litho.	n.d.
Giorgio de Chirico	*Calligrammes*	litho.	1930
Maurice Denis	*Thompson's Poems*	litho.	n.d.
Raoul Dufy	*La Belle-enfant, ou L'Amour à quarante ans*	etch.	1930
Marie Laurencin	*La Princesse de Cleves*	aquatint	n.d.
Fernand Léger	*Les Illuminations*	litho.	1949
Jean Lurçat	*Mes Domaines*	wc.	1958
Alberto Magnelli	*Poésie de mots inconnus*	aquatint	1949
Aristide Maillol	*Daphnis Playing on his Pipe Shepherds and Dryad*	woodcut	1926
	Maidens Fill the Woodland	woodcut	1926
	L'Art d'aimer	woodcut	1935
	Plant Forms	woodcut	1937
Albert Marquet	*Images d'une petite ville arabe*	etch.	n.d.
André Masson	*Les Hain-Teny*	etch.	1956
Henri Matisse	*Pasiphae, chant de Minos*	linoleum cut	1944
Joan Miró	*La Bague d'Aurore*	etch.	1957
Georges Rouault	*Parades*	litho. & wc.	1938
André Dunoyer de Segonzac	*Les Georgiques*	etch.	1937-43
Sophie Taeuber-Arp	*Poésie de mots inconnus*	litho.	1949
René Pierre Tal Coat	*Poets, Painters and Sculptors*	litho.	n.d.

VII MISCELLANY (partial listing)

Giacomo Balla	Palette and 2 brushes		c. 1925
Umberto Boccioni	Palette		n.d.
Constantin Brancusi	*The Kiss*	ink and oil on eggshell	1953
Alexander Calder	*Yellow Circle*	rug	
Pablo Picasso	*Female Figure*	ceramic	
	Bull's Head	ceramic plate	
	Serrure	rug	
	Untitled	rug	
	Owl	ceramic	

VIII ANTIQUITIES (partial listing)

Pre-Columbian: group of 11 stone and ceramic pieces of Aztec and Tarascan origin

Etrusco-Corinthian	Oil Flask	terra cotta	c. 6th Century B.C.
Roman	Capital	stone	3-1st Century B.C.
Egyptian	Amulet of two fingers	stone	date uncertain
Cypriot	Figurine	terra cotta	8-7th Century B.C.
Etruscan	Cinerary urn	stone	5-4th Century B.C.
Anatolian	Bird	bronze	end of 2nd Millenium B.C.

Photographic Credits

Black and white illustrations:

Detroit Institute of Arts: nos. 64, 103, 112, 114, 116, 117, 152, 157, 166, 188, 190, 193, 199, 207, 220, 228, 230, 232

Lew Gilcrest Studios, Birmingham: nos. 10, 13, 18, 22, 40, 48, 53, 70, 93, 99, 102, 105, 106, 168, 169, 176, 191, 192, 197, 205

Joseph Klima, Jr., Detroit: nos. 1, 12, 16, 19, 31, 33, 39, 50, 51, 56, 63, 67, 72, 74, 76-80, 83, 86-89, 93, 94, 98, 100, 107, 108, 111, 133, 134, 177, 214

Courtesy Dr. and Mrs. Barnett Malbin, Birmingham: nos. 2, 5, 7, 9, 11, 12, 14, 15, 17, 20, 24, 27-31, 35, 37, 38, 42, 44-47, 49, 52, 55a, 55b, 57, 62, 65, 66, 68, 71, 75, 81, 82, 85, 91, 101, 104, 109, 119, 138, 141, 142, 150, 151, 153, 162, 182, 187, 195, 196, 200, 201, 209, 215, 218, 223, 224, 229

Milwaukee Art Center: no. 6

Robert E. Mates and Susan Lazarus, New York: nos. 3, 4, 8, 21, 25, 34, 36, 41, 43, 54, 58, 60, 69, 73, 92, 95, 97, 110

Color Plates:

Joseph Klima, Jr., Detroit: nos. 26, 59, 102
Courtesy Dr. and Mrs. Barnett Malbin, Birmingham: no. 61
Robert E. Mates and Susan Lazarus, New York: nos. 23, 32, 84, 90, 96, 108

Supplementary Photographs:

Joseph Klima, Jr., Detroit: p. 27
Baltazar Korab, Birmingham: pp. 5, 17
Courtesy Dr. and Mrs. Barnett Malbin, Birmingham: pp. 6, 8, 15, 18, 20, 22, 28

Exhibition 73/5

3750 copies of this catalogue designed by Malcolm Grear
have been printed by the Meriden Gravure Company
in September 1973 for The Trustees of The Solomon R.
Guggenheim Foundation on the occasion of the exhibition
Futurism: A Modern Focus